16.00

Defying

the Darkness

Defying

the Darkness

...

Gay Theology in the Shadows

J. Michael Clark

RESOURCE *Publications* • Eugene, Oregon

Grateful acknowledgment is made for use of the following:
Reprinted by permission from *A Feminist Ethic of Risk* by Sharon D. Welch,
copyright © 1990 Augsburg Fortress. From *Making the Connections* by Beverly
Wildung Harrison. Copyright © 1985 by Beverly Wildung Harrison and Carol
S. Robb. Reprinted by permission of Beacon Press.

Biblical quotations are from the New Revised Standard Version of the Bible, ©
1989 by the Division of Christian Education of the National Council of the
Churches of Christ in the U.S.A., and are used by permission

Resource Publications
A division of Wipf and Stock Publishers
199 W 8th Ave, Suite 3
Eugene, OR 97401

Defying the Darkness
Gay Theology in the Shadows
By Clark, J. Michael
Copyright©1997 Pilgrim Press
ISBN 13: 978-1-60899-204-1
Publication date 11/12/2009
Previously published by Pilgrim Press, 1997

In memory of
Thelma Medlin Clark Morrison,
6 June 1905–6 August 1995,
for embodying tenacity and strength;

. . .

for all those whom
we have lost to HIV/AIDS,
for embodying courage and perseverance;

. . .

and
to my beloved spouse,
Bob McNeir,
for embodying grace and love in relation.

Contents

Naming the Demons

Life isn't safe. Certainly, life in the post-Holocaust, post-death-of-God, post-Christian, postmodern end of the twentieth century isn't safe. As the millennium approaches, long-denied demons demand our attention, anxious angels want wrestling, sleep is fitful and frightening. We wonder what is real and what is imagined, what is literal and what is metaphor. So unsafe, our lives feel scripted like some badly written, apocalyptic, horror B-movie. And theology trembles: How long has it been this way? When did the ground completely disappear beneath our feet? How are we to live with the terror? Survive the horror? Examining my own life, now, I wonder . . .

My senior year in high school followed the expansion of the Vietnam War into Cambodia and the brutal slaughter of students at Kent State University. The war was in our living room every night, all too vividly portrayed as Walter Cronkite shared the dinner hour with us. That school year ended with graduation from high school, entry into college, and one of the last national draft lotteries. My number was a perilous and premonitory seventeen, promising an unwanted journey to the jungles of Southeast Asia.

My dreamwork throughout that year made the horrors of Vietnam more personal than either dinnertime television or that threatening lottery number. My psyche managed to transpose my circle of friends from our local church youth group into the action images from newscasts. My friends and I were in those jungles, huddled in rain-soaked trenches, terrified while shells whizzed overhead. I awoke one night in uncontrollable tears because my family's cocker spaniel had gotten away from us kids in the trenches, only to be shot by the Vietcong. Inconsolable, I awakened as I carried his limp, warm body back to our camp. Strange juxtapositions, yes, but very real emotions of fear and loss. The terror and pain I felt were so real that they remain vivid memories a quarter-century later.

Ultimately, it was neither my application for conscientious objector status nor my registration for a preministerial deferment, but rather a medical disqualification based on a childhood illness that circumvented the looming specter of that seventeen and thereby prevented the lived realization of my nightmares. I had managed to escape this body count which claimed tens of thousands of my generation.

Now, decades later, I am amazed and saddened by the nightmares that become real for some of my students—one student's fiancé killed by his own brother in an argument just before midterm, another student's journal replete with memories of the violence her family fled in southern California, yet another student's apartment burglarized twice during one academic quarter. Atlanta is certainly no safe haven from neighborhood or gang violence. The terror seems everywhere around us some days. Newspapers, television news, police drama programs, movies, and novels seem to recount and, all too often, to relish a very high level of interpersonal violence. This almost suggests that violence itself has a life of its own, more insidious and more ubiquitous than the mere individuals responsible for creating and enacting it.

For those of us who are gay men and lesbians, our lives on the margins and at the edges have also become locations for violence, both in physical actions of gaybashing and in the subtler actions of homophobic prejudice, discrimination, and exclusion. In addition to the human violence perpetrated upon many of us, we have also come to realize another kind of terror, another kind of violence, one within our own embodied lives—HIV/AIDS. Not surprisingly perhaps, fear of HIV/AIDS and AIDS-related death and concern about AIDS-related ignorance and discrimination recur as frequent themes in my students' papers almost as often as they do in the daily lives of many gay men. Even though my spouse, Bob, and I are essentially healthy at this writing—free of any symptoms or other physical experience of HIV—our daily regimens of medications and routinely scheduled doctor appointments constantly remind us. The numbers games of T-cell counts, T-cell percentages, viral activity, and other blood work belie our good health. The several dozen friends and loved ones who are no longer with us because of AIDS also remind us by their absence: This terror is real.

No, life isn't safe. I escaped one body count for my generation only to come face to face with a life-threatening enemy I may not escape so easily. That horror is intimately near—in my very bodyself.

Doing theology isn't safe either. Theological activity undertaken by those of us marginalized both by academia and by institutional religion is a dangerous activity. Articulating theology and ethics in the face of antigay/antilesbian violence and HIV/AIDS is a fearful activity, an unexpected and unwise activity, a very queer thing to be engaged in at all. Running headlong into the darkness of homophobia and HIV/AIDS, gay liberation theology is fraught with dangers from within as well as from without: The dynamic activity of gay theology and ethics is imperiled by its own postmodernist and liberationist concerns to include everyone and to speak for no one. However valuable and, indeed, necessary these concerns may be, our efforts to nurture radical inclusivity and to avoid any exclusionary universalizations have created a veritable minefield for our theology. When we navigate that minefield without sufficient caution, we risk either hurting those whose lives we hoped to heal and liberate or having our work degenerate into some vacuous political correctitude.

We have to remember that the ethical demand in our liberation theology to celebrate diversity and to nurture collaborative solidarity is not a simplistic demand for political correctness. Merely inoffensive speech may miss deeper ethical issues; it may deny, without appropriate reflection, attitudes and feelings enculturated in us with which we must reckon. Although we cannot divorce ourselves from our social and ecological locations and certain of the irrational feelings deeply ingrained in us as a result, we must nevertheless attempt to name and defuse those feelings; we must certainly refuse to speak or to act out prejudicial attitudes. Charlotte Bunch has elaborated on this concern, noting that political correctness "often has a moralistic [or self-righteous] tone that implies if you do all the 'right' things, then you can wash your hands of responsibility for being part of an oppressive culture. But there is no way to deny that responsibility, no matter how correct one's personal behavior [or speech]. There is, however, the possibility of being ethical or taking responsibility for doing whatever one can about society."[1]

One means of taking ethical responsibility and thereby avoiding the pitfalls of exclusion or vacuous political correctitude increasingly has become that of naming our social and ecological locations, describing the contexts from which we speak as completely and thoroughly as we can.[2] Then we raise our voices with fewer presuppositions, fewer hidden agendas, in such a way that our voices are equal in relation and in power with the other voices that join with us in theological and ethical conversation.[3] There is, of course, a danger here as well—the risk that, ultimately, we will speak only for ourselves. Richard Rubenstein anticipated this dilemma long ago when he insisted: "Though theology purports to make statements about God, its significance rests on what it reveals about the theologian." Rubenstein explains that all theologies are inherently subjective, being statements about the way in which the theologian experiences the world, communicating an inner world that the theologian suspects others may share.[4]

To preclude having our subjectivity degenerate into mere solipsism, we can instead follow through on this suspicion that, at the very least, some other people do share our concerns—however partially they may do so. Then our theological subjectivity, our specifically located speech, can be understood not as gross universalization or as egotistical polemic, but as an invitation to dialogue, an invitation to relation.[5] In other words, we must assume the risks of honestly and forthrightly proclaiming who we are in such a way that our voices can be heard clearly as we participate in theological and ethical dialogue with an integrity that goes beyond mere political correctitude.

In my own previous writings, I have attempted to do just that at some length. Here again, I must reiterate that my theology emerges from my particular location as a monogamously coupled, white gay male southerner and an HIV-positive liberation theologian, one committed to pro-feminist theory and pro-earth practice, and one marginalized by both academia and religious institutions.[6] Those concerns that trouble me most deeply at this writing stem from my position as a gay man in relation to other gay and lesbian persons and our sometimes shared subculture or "community" and, more specifically still, as a gay man living with HIV/AIDS—in the embodied lives of friends living and dead, in the embodied life of the one man whom I love most dearly, and in my own embodied life. The dissonance between my spouse's and my own current health (for which we are very grateful) and our naysaying immune-system markers further shapes my perspective on this reality, while it also further nurtures my fears of the unknown. While our medical reports insist that there is a horror intimately indwelling in our very selves, our hearts and minds grapple with our fears, our uncertainties, and our determined efforts to live as so-called long-term survivors. Specifically for me as a theologian, this dissonance, this unnerving confusion, has compelled me over and over again to reconsider the question of suffering, traditionally phrased as the problem of evil or theodicy, and to revisit my own previous efforts to create meaning in the midst of oftentimes horrific uncertainty. It has also meant (as HIV/AIDS does for many of us) finding and refinding ways to affirm life and, indeed, to live life in the most accountable manner possible. It means insisting on life, and life lived well, even in the face of potential suffering and death. In short, I am confronted with both theodicy and ethics and the connections between the two, virtually every day.

One way in which Bob and I together have responded to the confusion and fears associated with HIV/AIDS has been to act very queerly indeed, to act contrary to conventional wisdom. Instead of sending us scurrying, frightened, in opposite directions, the discovery of my HIV-positive status and the beginning of Bob's AZT therapy early in 1990 only served to deepen our then year-old commitment to each other. We moved from a small apartment to a rented house and bought a car together, underscoring our physical commitment with a fiscal one. These events also served as the occasion for an earlier book in which we jokingly promised that, when we both required therapeutic intervention, we would find a crystal candy dish for our shared medication(s) and set the thing defiantly on the coffee table![7] Then, as friends continued to fall around us, and as our more negative friends and family members prematurely planned for our demise, queerly contrary to reason again, we took on a thirty-year mortgage and bought a house, creating an ecosystem of humans, dogs, birds, fishpond, and flower and vegetable gardens. Instead of dying, we immersed ourselves in a web of life-sustaining relationships: We became involved in our neighborhood watch and its leadership; we joined an AIDS-related service organization; I traded in my brown thumb for a green one in order to raise flowers and shape our yard; and Bob learned to grow and can vegetables, to make jams and jellies, and to duplicate and improve on our grandmothers' recipes. Time passed, and our numbers steadily changed. By late 1995 the need for that candy dish, for swallowing our fears on a daily schedule, coincided with the development and writing of another book—this book. Our continuing engagement in home and neighborhood, in work and volunteerism, in friendships and familial relationships still nurtures our queer defiance against the naysayers, even when those fears are hardest to swallow, even when those periodic daily reminders are scariest. And, even if it is queerly contrary to conventional wisdom, we continue to insist, both in our theory and in our practice, that HIV/AIDS does not have to be a death sentence.

Now from within this particular location, I find theology growing queerer, too. During the years between planning and purchasing our candy dish, "queer" became a verb as well as an adjective. "Queer theory" and the "queer theology" that developed alongside gay liberation theology (the former more brash and loud than the latter) has used "queer" to transgress, to turn established orders upside down and inside out, to defy conventional reason and established tradition. "To queer" is to say "no" to anything and everything that denies the fullness of life to gay men and lesbians or to those living with HIV/AIDS. "To queer" is to turn an epithet on its head, to shout down the silence that equals death.[8]

Belatedly accepting this defiant, transgressive label for my own theological process, I realize now that Bob's and my life together—promising to live to be crotchety old men who one day, decades hence, will burn our mortgage together—is a transgressive action. Having to wrestle with theodicy and ethics and HIV/AIDS and their particular interconnectedness is transgressive, queer praxis. The conflation of my particular embodied life and my peculiar theological pilgrimage demand not only querying the Divine one more time, but also defying or "queering" the darkness, defying the AIDS apocalypse in our midst. For me, such queersome activity means not only pushing the limits of theodicy to affirm life in the face of death, but going even further to articulate what it means to live that life as an ethical life, to queerly envision living with HIV/AIDS for the long haul—perhaps even to imagine what it might be like to live beyond AIDS, after AIDS. And, that's the queerly beckoning light behind the horrific darkness of theodicy at the AIDS-riddled end of the present millennium.

Unlike my own compelling confrontation with the problem of theodicy in response to HIV/AIDS—unlike what I experience or what I have expected others to experience—a very dear friend and colleague, Richard Hardy, has argued that gay men living with HIV/AIDS do not actually struggle much with theodicy.[9] I find it queerly ironic, therefore, that Hardy's description of the spiritual impasse these men experience is such a perfect metaphor for the struggle with theodicy that I have experienced, not as some final answer or spiritual endpoint, but rather as a nonanswer that initiates a necessary passage, something we must go through to be more fully engaged in life. According to Hardy, reaching an impasse or dark night of the soul about one's HIV status holds the "potential for transformation and the discovery of the authentic, whole self," provided that one enters "into the experience rather than giving up or running away from it"; moreover, "an impasse can transform us only when our yielding is an active surrender with all the risk which that entails . . . and an affirmation of hope which dares to live out whatever the experience contains for the person in the present moment [and] a determination to live out whatever it will hold in the future."[10] I would contend that confronting and pushing through the impasse of theodicy, wrestling with the horror and tragedy in our tradition and in our very embodied lives, has the same queerly transformative potential. Hardy argues, for example, that the "insight of impasse" is "that despite the apparent emptiness and hopelessness, God is there with us, closer than ever before," a realization that enables deeper self-acceptance and self-accountability, a more meaningful life in the very face of death, and "a commitment to live life in an increasingly constructive way."[11]

While we penetrate the impasse of HIV/AIDS and enter into and through the dark night of wrestling with theodicy's enigmatic angel, by degrees (when our first friend dies; as friends' deaths accumulate; when we or our spouses become HIV-positive, start prophylactic medication, or even reach full-blown AIDS), our commitments to life and to living are embodied in how we ride out the ups and downs of T-cell counts, medical protocols and their occasional side effects, or even periodic opportunistic infections. Our commitments to all of life are embodied in our living with and through our fears to embrace our position on the margins as the location where we also embrace our special loved ones, our personal ecosystems, and life itself.

Taking Hardy's work one step further, then, I would contend also that, just as we cannot run away from our mortality, neither can we circumvent a confrontation with the issues and questions raised by theodicy. Moreover, I believe we can find in that confrontation not an ending, but a passage, a process that discloses a very important insight in theodicy's enigmatic nonanswer: The real issue is not why or what comes after, but "What do I do now, and who is there to help me do it?"[12]

When we (re)assume responsibility in the wake of the death of any and every rescuing god or *deus ex machina,* we can discover the divine empowerment and sustenance in the very midst of seeming godforsakenness that enables us to move beyond self-pity and the fear of death. Once so unencumbered, we can discover yet further empowerment for the queerly defiant tasks of living our lives as embodiments that matter, even as we seek to enhance the quality of life for every life and for life itself. To live in such a fashion is also to live as embodiments of justice, or as what feminist and profeminist theology commonly refer to as embodiments of justice as right relation. In other words, through confronting death and nevertheless committing ourselves to life, we can also discover in that process the empowerment both to discern and to live an ethical life in relation to all that is.

This book is about that journey; it is an invitation to explore together that movement through the horrors of querying the Divine toward the queer defiance of defying the darkness with our tenacious, accountable, and ethical lives, both in relation to ourselves and in relation to all life. It is an activity fittingly crafted at winter's solstice, as we endure the increasing darkness, queerly hoping and believing in the rebirth of that light which will gradually lead us toward a new spring.[13]

$\mathcal{U}$ndermining the Theological Ground

As I have wrestled anew with the demons of darkness—the terrors of theodicy that have plagued my embodied spiritual confrontation with HIV/AIDS—and as I have reached out for some solid, safe grounding to escape those fears, I have become increasingly aware of the fragile, shaky quality of the ground on which we construct theology in the late twentieth century. That frightening awareness also has led me to a closely related and strange discovery: I do theology within our two-pronged Judeo-Christian tradition with very little recourse to its sacred scriptures. In fact, I studiously avoid the Bible whenever I can. Instead, over the course of a decade or more, I have developed an ever-expanding canon of feminist, profeminist, and gay-affirmative books and articles which I believe to be the most reliable resources for my work in post-Christian and profeminist gay theology and ethics. I've realized that to the extent these trustworthy resources sometimes function as secondary sources in relation to our tradition's scriptures, then my own work emerges as a tertiary layer of theological reflection and dialogue. Interestingly enough, had I not been invited to serve on an "ideological criticism" panel in the Society of Biblical Literature (SBL) in 1992, I might have remained essentially unreflective about the ascriptural nature of my theological resources for some time to come. As it turned out, my preparations for that panel enabled me to discern four potential basic resources for, or locations of, theological authority: (1) in scrip-

ture and the canon; (2) in the community of faith, whether Jewish or
Christian; (3) in the institutions and institutionalized expressions and
traditions of such a community; and, (4) in the experience of people,
particularly in the experience of those persons who have been
oppressed by any of the other forms of religious expression and praxis.
The experience of life at the margins, or on the edge (the fourth
resource), virtually undermines any authoritativeness in the other three
potential theological resources. In other words, particularly for those of
us who are gay men and lesbians in the primarily Christian West, our
experience of oppression by much of the canon, scriptural interpretation and tradition, and church and synagogue becomes our authoritative standpoint for appraising all of the other basic resources.[1]

As a gay theologian approaching biblical studies, for example, I am
painfully aware of the extent to which the Bible has been used, over and
over again, as a tool of oppression and even terrorism, as the ideological
justification not only for excluding gay men and lesbians, but also for
blaming the victim in the AIDS health crisis and for engaging in acts of
antigay/antilesbian violence. I am equally aware that the biblical mandate in Genesis to have dominion over the earth has more often been
read as domination, thus making the Bible a sanction for the exploitation of the earth. In short, persons carrying floppy Bibles, as if they
were some sort of weapon, evoke passionate emotions in me—especially fear. By elucidating these realizations, I recognize that I am coming
out of the closet again, this time as a theologian who is also a scripture-
phobe. And, more difficult still, I have to try to make sense of my scripture-phobia and to ask myself what it means. In reckoning with these
issues as early as 1989, I had written:

> A "closed canon" of scripture and a narrow, male-restricted ecclesiastical
> authority over doctrine and tradition have forced feminist theologians to
> reject even attempting to "read themselves into" accumulated, canonized
> (and hence closed) religious experience. Gay theology must do likewise....
> Our very exclusion, whether as women or as gay people, becomes a criti-
> cism of scripture and tradition. Revaluing minority experience, therefore,
> means penetrating [and] resolving the conflict of experience and tradi-
> tion by forcibly reopening the canon.[2]

In other words, our experience of oppression and exclusion provides us with a "hermeneutic of suspicion," which we are bound to apply to scripture and canon, to institution and tradition, alike.[3] A hermeneutic of suspicion becomes the liberation theologian's criterion of selectivity for dismissing outright *any* oppressive elements in, and for choosing to focus on the prophetic strands of, our scriptures and our traditions. Even then—and particularly because it so often seems only a minority voice with little efficacy against the oppressive, majoritarian status quo—the prophetic tradition in scripture is at best *illustrative*, not *authoritative* per se. Granted, drawing on the prophetic tradition in scripture in an artifactual manner has a certain rhetorical force. However, even given its illustrative power, it is not the scripture that holds authority; it is the standpoint of oppression and the concomitant demand of justice that are authoritative.

A hermeneutic of suspicion also leads me to an ideological suspicion. I am increasingly convinced that there is no such thing as pure objectivity, and certainly no purely objective biblical criticism. Because all approaches to scripture entail certain presuppositions, putative objectivity is itself an ideology, a heterosexist ideology most often used to maintain the oppressive methodologies of the majority over against the oppressed. Elsewhere I have commented:

Academic ghettos define the scope of so-called legitimate scholarship and craft a putative objectivity that brackets any creative diversity of methodologies and subjects into categories of "alternative life styles" and thereby protects heterosexist literary criticism, religious studies, sociology, and other disciplines from intellectual "contamination." . . .

If staying safely within the confines of . . . the academically acceptable . . . only furthers ghettoization and too narrow vision, the risk of offending these myopic standards must be assumed by the gay liberation theologian.[4]

My hermeneutic of suspicion, including my suspicions about objectivity, further lead me to ask whether the scriptures really have much of positive value to say to gay and lesbian experience. The Old Testament, for example, speaks pretty loudly to gay men in particular, and scriptural work here can be very dysfunctional. For example, we may argue that the Sodom and Gomorra story actually portrays a violent, heteropatriarchal culture and, within that context, a failure to fulfill hospitality norms. Or we may argue that this narrative even wrestles with the more specific issue of sexual violence, and thus that it is not really a biblical condemnation of homosexuality at all. Nevertheless, average churchgoers and mainstream white middle-Americans are likely to remain unconvinced. Likewise, while most people do not generally adhere to the holiness code, that code's condemnation of homosexuality as an abomination, in collusion with the Sodom and Gomorra story, forever will be used to motivate homophobia and antigay/antilesbian violence. Similarly, in the New Testament, we may find a variety of ways to contextualize, explain, or otherwise mitigate Paul's exclusion of gay male *and* lesbian sexuality, but I do not believe we ever will find a way to clearly make the Pauline corpus progay! Granted, we do find certain possibly homoerotic images in the Bible, such as the same-sex love of David and Jonathan, or Ruth and Naomi, or even Jesus and John the Beloved. However comforting these images may be at some level, they nevertheless seem incidental, artifactual, and merely conveniently comforting asides for gay men and/or lesbians, but asides with no particular message or authority.

. . .

Disturbing Beginnings: Creation

. . .

Just as I find that the scriptures are neither authoritative nor particularly informative for gay/lesbian being, relationships, or liberation, so also do I question their value for recent efforts to include the larger global context of our human lives in our reflective field of vision and thereby also to include ecological accountability in our theology and ethics. I have been especially struck, for example, by how both male and feminist writers in ecology and religion have struggled with the early chapters of Genesis.

Anne Primavesi's efforts to salvage the creation narratives for the believing Christian lead her to affirm that although "the interpretation of the Genesis texts . . . which prevailed was a male construct bound by and acceptable to . . . a patriarchal culture and specific to a time when male consciousness was taken as the norm," nonetheless an ecofeminist alternative reading is also possible: "The integral relationship between sustenance, the difficulties of securing it, and human relations," all depicted as interwoven in Genesis, "are the interpretive grid through which, . . . ecology reminds us, this narrative has become relevant today."[5]

Another writer, James Nash, also wants to salvage the Genesis materials. Focusing not on the creation narratives but on the subsequent flood story, he insists that the Noahide covenant portrays the Divine as "making an unconditional pledge in perpetuity to all humanity, to all other creatures, and to the earth itself, to preserve *all* species and their environments." Moreover, because the "ecological covenant" entailed by the Noahide covenant "assumed responsibilities to future generations of humanity," ecological abuses in the present violate this ongoing covenant.[6]

In response to both Primavesi and Nash, I contend that any problems inherent in either of their views may be seen as the result of these writers' presuppositions—their assumption of an imputed authority in the Genesis materials. For example, to read Genesis 1–3 as a story of origins with at least two primary motifs—that male dominion, stewardship, or domination of nature is somehow divinely decreed, and that "original sin" came into human existence by means of putatively "evil" nature (represented by the serpent and imputed to all women)—clearly is to engage in a patriarchal, sexist, and even misogynist reading-back into a historical text. However, Primavesi's ecofeminist alternative— that in context the story is about the conditions of life at the time, the struggle for basic subsistence, and the paradox of a very difficult existence being given by a presumably loving God—may be wishful thinking. This is, at best, also a reading-back into the text, and, at worst, still a heterosexist reading. Even if the archetypal man and woman *are* created equal, the gender roles of procreative necessity are still a very significant part of the human survival message in this text, a dialectic which still pits (heterosexual) men and women together in a struggle with nature as resistant "other" in order for them to survive. Human domination of nature is still implicit, because the text's ideological bottom line is that humans are the pinnacle of creation and must survive, come what may. Genesis thus does not *clearly* present an ecologically sound view. And by virtue of its heterosexist assumption (however historically necessary it might be in context), it has little if anything to say to gay men and lesbians, except to remind us all of our inherent connection to the earth.

Rather than accept either Nash's or Primavesi's perspective here, I am more inclined to accept a third, more anecdotal perspective on the Genesis materials. In drawing together Torah, Talmud, and Midrash to weave his own personal commentary on the opening chapters of Genesis, Elie Wiesel raises the possibility that the Creator questioned the wisdom of making a human the center of creation.[7] To transpose current theological jargon onto Wiesel's reading, the Fall in Genesis becomes a cosmic action of decentering.

An important concept for liberation theology, decentering may be understood as the shifting, even the dismantling, of oppressive centers of "power-over." It dissolves heterosexist power, for example; it seeks to bring the margins and the marginalized from the margins to the center of our compassionate attention. However, for decentering to be genuinely meaningful for theology, it cannot be reduced to a simple exchange of margins to center and center to margins. Decentering cannot be a mere inversion of the center/margins hierarchy whereby those who were formerly oppressed now become the oppressors. Radical decentering entails far more than that. Indeed, the focus must be not just on shifting, but on dismantling the center: "Things fall apart; the center cannot hold."[8] In other words, decentering must mean exploding the very concept of centers of power and hierarchies of power-over. Power-over must be displaced by power-with.[9] As we then bring all that is to the center in a radical inclusivity of utterly equal and intrinsic value, the center itself dissipates and falls apart. Embracing all that is— both human and nonhuman, both biospheric and geospheric—dissolves the center/margins dichotomy.

Ultimately, in response to the question, "Do we *have* to resort to Genesis or to any scripture for a sound theological and ethical vision, for a gay-affirmative and earth-friendly theology and ethics?" we will affirm that we do not. Our experience of oppression and expendability, and of that reflected in our culture's attitudes of exploitation and disposability toward the earth, as well as our experience of God's intimate nearness and coempowerment with the oppressed are surer grounds for a gay theology of liberation. Given that assertion, then, the conclusion of the flood narrative *does* have at least anecdotal value for us: If gay men and lesbians are truly a "rainbow people," celebrating our own diversity (as signified by our rainbow flag) and celebrating the earth's diversity as well, then our encounter with and appreciation of the rainbow covenant in Genesis 9 remind us that we must not seek some other-worldly, ghettoized, "over the rainbow" panacea, but must instead honor the rainbow covenant in solidarity with all other oppressed persons, with God, and with the earth, intimately interrelated here and now.[10]

■ ■ ■

Discomforting Endings: Eschatology

■ ■ ■

Just as creation narratives are problematic for me, so are biblical materials at the other end of the scriptural spectrum. "Eschatology," for example, is certainly a theological term that requires a thoroughgoing deconstruction and reconstruction. Catherine Keller defines it generally as "discourse about the ultimate or the end . . . a temporal or spatial end, edge, or horizon." She defines "apocalypse" more specifically as a disclosure, revelation, or unveiling which creates vision or enables insight and which, as "the edgiest of eschatologies, always reveals the threat to a *particular* world."[11]

One insight in Keller's work has come through for me with increasing vividness: Our traditional understandings of eschatology—of death as not-death, *not really*—have had extremely negative human and environmental consequences. Traditional eschatology has functioned as yet one more sanction for devaluing and, ultimately, disvaluing the earth, this embodied life, and virtually all marginalized peoples—a situation that other feminist theologians have duly noted. While Sallie McFague, for example, insists that "the model of the human being seeking its own salvation . . . is not only anachronistic to our current sense of reality but dangerous," Rosemary Radford Ruether has even more pointedly said that "by pretending that we can immortalize ourselves, souls and bodies, we are immortalizing our garbage and polluting the earth."[12] Elsewhere, Keller has explained further that the "drive to transcendent unity" with the Divine, outside or beyond this life and this world, is "a profound impetus in all patriarchal spirituality, and it always achieves its end at the expense of nature and multiplicity."[13] Devaluing this earth inevitably leads to the careless disvaluing of the diversity of life on earth, by means of exclusion and/or exploitation, to the point of extinction. Eliminating diversity and complexity—among both human and nonhuman life—works toward eliminating *any* viable future for life on earth. Sadly, of course, this is a matter of little concern to those who are spiritually otherworldly and apocalyptically minded. As Keller also observes: "Apocalypticism portrays the death of everything as the way to the eternal life of the privileged few."[14]

The real danger beneath such transcendent, eschatological spirituality becomes frighteningly clear: Not only does such spirituality disvalue and disdain the earth and all religiously excluded lives, human and nonhuman, but the linear thinking that informs such spirituality actually looks forward to the total demise of the earth! The danger of patriarchal, linear thinking is that it assumes both a literal beginning ("creation") and a literal ending ("eschaton"). Coupled with a transcendent, otherworldly spirituality, such linear thinking can also be understood to imply that we *can* or that we *should* work the earth toward that end and thereby hasten the arrival of the "next" world. Such otherworldliness not only devalues and disvalues this world, but actually sanctions exhausting a clearly expendable earth! In response to such thinking, therefore, Keller not only has acknowledged that "the expectation of an end-time and of an end of time has . . . defined the limits of western patriarchal consciousness," but also has realized that neither "scientific modernity" with its seemingly endless exploitation of expendable "resources" nor religious apocalypticism "reflects the spatiotemporal rhythms of earthly ecology."[15]

Carol Johnston offers one alternative to such a frightening eschatology when she reconceptualizes the final depiction of apocalypticism in scripture, envisioning *not* a linear endpoint, but a present image by means of which we might (re)construct our praxis. She argues that the apocalypse as depicted in Revelation 21–22 portrays the Divine as coming to dwell with people on earth. Rather than forsaking the earth as an expendable commodity, her view affirms the earth as the locus of intimate and healing divine presence and companionship: "In this vision, it is not earth that will be abandoned, but heaven. . . . This is a metaphorical vision of shalom, imaging a world of restored trust. God, human beings, and earth are reunited and dwell together in peace [with] the flourishing diversity of creation."[16] Whether such hopeful scriptural reconstruction and revisioning can counter popular, disposable-style eschatology is, of course, an open question. That issue notwithstanding, Keller and biblical scholar Tina Pippin have both reexamined the biblical apocalypse in its politico-historical context, from a liberationist perspective. Keller argues, for example, that "the habit of transcendence upwards . . . seems to be a symptom of systemic suffering . . . from which selves can find no earthly relief."[17] In other words, according to Pippin, an apocalypse like the one so vividly described in Revelation may be understood as the last desperate vision generated by an oppressed people who no longer can imagine achieving justice for themselves in the present realities of this world. Apocalypse then becomes not so much a creative vision of faith as an acknowledgment of failure, a final relinquishing of hope in the here and now.[18]

While the horrors of the Johannine revelation may first appear as only so many historical artifacts, modern life is actually replete with clear examples of apocalypses generated by collective despair. As but one example, the Ghost Dance spirituality which emerged throughout the American Indian nations in the 1880s and which inadvertently precipitated the violence of Wounded Knee in 1890 is another vivid example of this-worldly hopelessness transformed into apocalyptic hopes.[19] No doubt the self-fulfilling apocalypticism of Jim Jones, David Koresh, and their followers also fits within this tradition, albeit nurtured more by theological than sociopolitical despair. From yet another, quite different perspective within the context of gay liberation theology, one

cannot help but wonder if any capitulation to AIDS fear or any resignation to AIDS itself (any too easy acceptance of HIV exposure, progression, and ultimately AIDS death) on the part of some gay men, or the
disproportionate suicide rate particularly among gay/lesbian adoles-
cents, is not an enactment of apocalyptic despair on the part of those
gay people who no longer can envision an end to the theocratic politics
of homophobia and antigay/antilesbian oppression and violence. An
AIDS death and a place on the Names Project memorial quilt become
the only remaining heroic means of escape from culturally induced low
self-esteem and internalized self-hatred. By embodying their own
expendability in death, these victims of AIDS apocalypticism also
embody the attitudes of fatalistic abandonment which at least portions
of our western culture and its traditional, scripturally based eschatology
continue to enact toward putatively disposable people and an exploited,
expendable earth.

To her credit, Keller provides us with yet another alternative to both
otherworldly and politically desperate eschatologies. She argues that we
must come "to understand ultimacy in terms of the primacy of the
inhabited earth" and that "our responsibility for the new creation . . . is
to participate in our finite, interconnected creatureliness with metanoic
consciousness."[20] While "the indifference toward nature implied in traditional eschatology becomes lethal—that is, its distraction from the
earth complies in the destruction of the earth," a more responsible
eschatology in contrast must be "an ecologically sound eschatology, one
that motivates work to save our planet"—which is to say, an apocalyptic
unveiling or insight that reveals hope and that creates visions of a
future toward which we are empowered to work in the present, here
and now.[21] Our insights or moments of revelation (our apocalypses)
must motivate us to rewrite eschatology and thereby to change our
vision of linear ends by reenvisioning renewal and restoration within
the cycles of earthly life. Such revelations should disclose hope and
empowerment for corrective change and human liberation—hope that
precludes apocalyptic despair.

Clearly, biblical work around both gay/lesbian liberation and environmental issues either fails to speak to us at all or does so in a merely artifactual way. Or worse, its often frightening ideologies keep us so mired

in argumentative apologetics that we accomplish nothing. The old ruse of proving anything or any position with the Bible is fairly easily done when applied to everyday life, particularly the everyday life of the oppressed, whether oppressed people or an exploited earth. With but a few artifactual exceptions, scripture cannot be made to support gay and lesbian liberation and more often has been used as a tool of oppression against us or as a mandate for domination and exploitation against the earth. That is why I am scripture-phobic.

But if scripture, as a resource for our theology, is not authoritative or often even reliable, where can we find resources that are? I come back to reaffirming that, although not ultimately authoritative and certainly not in any oppressive way, the prophetic tradition heavily seasoned with a "hermeneutic of suspicion" and the experience of oppression altogether constitute the surest grounding for the activity of doing gay liberation theology and ethics. Given the uncertainty and sometimes terror of life in the late 1990s, however—particularly for gay men and lesbians and all persons living with HIV/AIDS—the marriage of the prophetic tradition and our experience remains frighteningly shaky ground for theological activity. Life between creation and eschatology, between birth and death, remains a scary and tenuous journey.

• • •

Dysfunctional Middles: Fear and Suffering

• • •

As I have become fully cognizant of my own scripture-phobia (more aware of the dysfunctional messages in the tradition that scripture tenuously grounds and informs), I have also discovered a deeper, more profound phobia haunting not only the edges of my consciousness, but the very center of my life experience. Because I am not only a gay man, but someone who has been HIV-positive since early 1990 and someone whose spouse has been HIV-positive since 1987, my liberational commitments to this life and this-worldly justice have run headlong into a confrontation with human mortality in the middle of the AIDS health

crisis. The confluence of scripture-phobia, homophobia, and HIV/
AIDS-phobia raises the question: How do I resolve the very personal
confluence of sexual embodiment and mortality in my life, if I am to do
so informed by my own evolving theological reflections?

At one level, a thoroughly this-worldly alternative to otherworldly
hopes is very difficult to accept: Watching so many of our friends die
"due to complications from AIDS" before their fortieth birthdays, while
we monitor our own embodied selves and our health and immune systems, makes the idea that when we die, we are dead, period, end of sub-
ject(ivity), extremely unpalatable. On the personal level, while I know
both intellectually, theologically, and even ecologically that life and
death are one, that just as we came out of that oneness we must return
to it, and that any otherworldly eschatology is certainly ecologically
untenable, I am still deeply troubled by my own impending mortality as
well as that of those I love. I definitely do not want life to be over any
time soon; I do not want my subjective experience of my relational net-
work to come to an end.

When I worked on this issue during the early 1990s, I tried to argue
that (that is, I tried to convince myself that) if we open ourselves to life
with gratitude and meet death with appropriate grief, knowing that life
and death are really one, we can begin to take responsibility for our
dying as well as for our living. I argued that we are called into deep trust
that the same erotically empowered creative urge which birthed us
forth from unindividuated oneness, that same cosuffering companion
energy which urged us into right relation as individual embodiments
and which empowered our righteous anger whenever our phenomenal
selves encountered wrong relation or injustice, that same divine oneness awaits us as we sacrifice our individuality to return to the dynamic
cycles of death and life. In short, I concluded, nobody said it would be
easy. However, a sweet bye-and-bye eschatology is not only escapism; it
is an escapism that impugns the earth and damages life with reckless,
disvaluing disregard, and that, as a result, also threatens to deny the
value of our personal lives. Rather than have the value of our lives so
canceled out, I argued, we can embrace our gratitude and our grief—
our erotically embodied passions—and choose an absolutely trusting,
eschatological leap of faith. A hard and painful choice, it can also be a

liberating and empowering one, freeing us from a fearful obsession with death to being more fully alive in the present and to living proactively as if, indeed, there were no tomorrow.[22]

However, when I first began sharing these views in a series of three public lectures during 1993–94, my friend and colleague Ron Long questioned the seemingly passive, even Pollyanish acceptance of death and suffering he believed implicit in my remarks. His comments, coupled with my increasingly this-worldly commitments to gay liberation theology, compelled me to revisit this ever-unresolved theological dilemma. Long perceived correctly that, for the most part, I had resigned myself to a process-theological perspective, believing that God does all God can do in every instance, but also acknowledging that often this is far from sufficient. Such a deity is not responsible for evil or inbreaking chaos, but is often impotent to save us from its consequences. While Long clearly rejects the often judgmental, omni-everything deity of most traditional eschatology in his own published work on this subject, adamantly asserting that "it strains credibility . . . to suppose that a [G]od who would send AIDS could be trusted to provide a future even for the dead," he just as adamantly rejects the God of process when he says, "To speak of God in any way that would imply that God either 'sends' or even merely 'tolerates' AIDS is morally anathema."[23] He goes on to explain that, in essence, the problem with process theology is its emphasis on the deity as a Creator or cocreator. If God is in any sense Creator, Long argues, God is more than just *implicated* in the realities of evil, God is in fact *responsible* for its existence, and evil is justified as the acceptable price for created life. This, of course, Long finds unacceptable: Suffering and death as the acceptable barter for life on earth is absolutely *not* acceptable.[24]

In making a mental distinction, as a good process theologian should, between human evil and so-called natural evil, I attempted not only to circumvent Long's objections to process theology, but also to avoid blaming God for the failed and perverted human responsibility of the Holocaust, racial lynchings, and antigay/antilesbian violence. I agreed with Dietrich Bonhoeffer that we humans must assume responsibility maturely for our actions as if God did not exist, conceding that the Divine cannot and will not rescue us.[25] I argued that if God is a cocre-

ator, interwoven and interspersed throughout all that is from the beginning, and if God both cosuffers evil with us and empowers us to combat
it, then God is no longer responsible for it. But Long would not let me
off the hook: God—not as the creative origin or first cause, but as a
copartner, cocreating all along—is still implicated (read, "responsible")
in the whole business of lived reality as we know and suffer it.[26]

So, the question remains: "Why is there suffering at all?" Theologically and ecologically, I had come to see God as the whole web of being,
as the cycles of life/death/rebirth—which does clearly implicate the deity
in both life and death, and we have to live in that paradox. However, I
also had tried *not* to make God an anthropomorphically culpable moral
agent who either wills or allows our suffering. I had avoided assigning
moral culpability to God by always circling back to a process-informed,
cosuffering, and caring impotence, because it is very frightening to concede that there simply may be no answer to the question of theodicy.
And Long was again correct in pointing out that I had not allowed
myself to be angry about this state of theological and spiritual affairs.

Anger is in fact a hallmark of Long's AIDS theology. He argues, for
example, that "the life of clarity is . . . grounded in an anger with
oppressive victimization and issues in battle, as well as in a refusal of
complicity with victimization, evil, and death"; more specifically, "in
anguished indignation . . . we cry out that AIDS should never have been
or ever should exist" until finally our "anger passes over into compassion and resolve"—the resolve, above all, to deny AIDS the last word
and never to be "in complicity with the destruction that is AIDS."[27] Bor-
rowing from Brazilian theologian Rubem Alves, Long uses his invest-
ment in anger to shape a doctrine of God: "God is to be defined as that
reality which guarantees that our feelings of revulsion at any given evil
are more than . . . our parochial feelings," which implies, ironically in
cosuffering, processlike terms, that our "passionate protest over injustice and compassion for its victims is an echo of the divine pathos."[28] In
short, Long reconceptualizes the deity neither as Creator nor even as an
implicated (responsible) cocreator, but rather as the very energy of
righteous anger, the "spirit of resistance," and a "complex of anger,
resolve, and hope." He concludes that "we do not hope because we
believe—rather we believe because we hope," and that specifically,

"hope for life after AIDS is really but a cipher for a hope for life and more life."[29]

Long's commitment to anger as a theological hallmark and to resistance as the primary characteristic of the Divine, together bring him full circle in his critique of my process-theological position. He says in a footnote that "in opting for a 'process' theodicy . . . Clark compromises what I have long thought the genius of the Western tradition, the right to be in a lover's quarrel with the Divine."[30] My immediate response to Long's specific critique reflected my developing horizontal theological commitments: The Jobian right to engage in a "lover's quarrel" with the world order, the cosmos, or the Divine locks the faithful into an anthropocentric and argumentative mode, which in itself does nothing to facilitate corrective actions and, worse, ignores the nonhuman dimensions of life. Because this futile quarrel keeps us focused on the human to the neglect of all other life on earth, the lover's quarrel with God is a myopic, even antiecological posture; whereas an alternative standpoint that realizes the limitations or "impotence" of God to rescue humans, even persons with AIDS (PWAs), compels us to (re)assume responsibility for action, for justice-making and caregiving, in both the human and nonhuman arenas.[31]

Despite these early misgivings with Long's critical perspective, our informal conversations on these matters ultimately compelled me to make one important concession: I have a problem with getting angry. Even though I have become more adept over the years at being angry in constructive, activist ways around both gay/lesbian and environmental issues, I have continued to fear getting angry at God. My southern Protestant upbringing taught me it wasn't *nice* to be angry. Indeed, in many southern families, we are so busy being *nice* that we never get angry, and we never work through that anger to richer levels of intimacy in relation. Instead, anger turns inward to become resentment, or depression and low self-esteem, while our relationships are constituted by shallow pleasantries and distance rather than by passionate confrontation and compassionate intimacy. And, of course, if one is not allowed to be angry at another person, one certainly is not allowed to be angry at God. That really wouldn't be *nice*, and the angry person would probably go to hell!

Well, suffering *is* hell; a long and lingering AIDS death is hell; griev-ing homophobic oppression and antigay/antilesbian violence year after year is hell; losing dozens and dozens of our friends to AIDS is hell. And we should be mad as hell. I should be. Long's comments reminded me that, particularly in the Jewish side of my mixed bag of faith develop-ment, our tradition says it's okay to get mad at the Divine. I have learned to trust the intimate relationship with my spouse to the extent that I can be angry with him or he can be angry with me, and yet we know we still love each other. I must learn to have no less faith in my relationship to the Divine.[32] But that is a very scary act of faith, one nei-ther passive nor Pollyanish.

Elie Wiesel has articulated well this aspect of my dilemma in his marvelous play, *The Trial of God,* wherein the evil of pogroms and the righteousness of protest are played out.[33] Wiesel reminds us that to deny the existence of the Divine because of suffering and death implies a kind of answer to theodicy, when in fact no answer may exist and "everything remains hidden."[34] Likewise, there are times when trying to separate human evil and so-called natural evil, to focus on human responsibility and to soften our anger at the Divine just does not work. Reminding us that *both* kinds of evil implicate God, Wiesel's protesting innkeeper, Berish, declares: "Every man who suffers or causes suffer-ing, every woman who is raped, every child who is tormented impli-cates" the Divine.[35] *Both the gaybasher and AIDS implicate God.* Through the character of Berish, Wiesel wisely articulates both our questions and our frustrations: We desperately want a comprehensible answer to theodicy, a conception of divine justice that makes sense to our everyday understandings of what justice means; but, no such answer comes.[36] God conceptualized as a neutral bystander to suffering is not enough; neither is an impotent, limited, process deity.[37] Can we then find any satisfaction in seeing God as less present in the causes of suffering and more present as an advocate of the victims of suffering?[38] Will an empathetic and cosuffering, but basically powerless, deity work to skirt theodicy? Does the divine impotence of process theology still imply a kind of divine complicity in evil? Or, do we, Joblike, have any better reality from which to choose?

The god of the whirlwind did not *really* answer Job. But both the Job-writer and Wiesel (as well as Long) insist that protest against the nonanswer is the only response that allows us both our dignity and our humanity. As Berish puts it, "I have not opted for God. I'm against [God's] enemies, that's all."[39] In fact, to defend our traditional concepts of an all-powerful, all-loving, all-knowing deity—one whose justice is not ours to understand—may well be to play into the hands of evil itself. In the play's surprising final action, Wiesel reminds us that God and Satan are in cahoots, tormenting Job. The defender of God is unmasked as the devil himself, reiterating the innkeeper's truth that protest is the *real* act of faith.[40] While my scripture-phobia is only worsened by the nonanswer of Job, my terror only deepened by Wiesel's final unmasking of God/Satan, both Long's critique and Wiesel's dramatic presentation helped me to begin to rearticulate my own approach to theodicy. They helped me to know which questions to ask and to realize there are far more questions than answers. They also have helped me to know how to be angry, how to protest, and thereby how to begin acting in faith rather than fear.

To lament the absence of God as rescuer from suffering and tragedy also entails protesting that abandonment. Grief actually entails anger and protest toward the reality that this is just the way it is—period. Anger and grief go hand in hand, as they do for the child who has temporarily lost his or her parents in a large store and feels abandoned by them. Our unanswered lament (our plea and our protest) in the face of that abandonment and in the face of the negatives of life (suffering) both heightens the preciousness of life's goods and undermines our experience of thanksgiving for those goods: How can we be grateful to one who abandons us? Is God only a fair-weather friend? Or is God really not there at all? How do we direct our prayers—whether of gratitude or anger—to an amorphous, ecologically whole web of being? We are left again with the paradoxical mixture of both gratitude (as joy and thanksgiving) and grief (as mourning and angry protest) before a reality we cannot change and without any answerable, theistic being. The faith required for protest is certainly no easier than the faith required for an eschatological leap of faith. I do not want to be separated from life and relationships and nature and God. But if the cycles of life/death, inter-woven with/in/to the whole web of being (an ecological divine oneness), are all there is and if in death there is no subjective experience of these separations, what does my resisting mortality mean except that I do not want these experiences to end? Ultimately, all of these unanswered (and unanswerable?) questions lead to one very important realization: Because all of our lives are interrelated, my passing into nonbeing will not invalidate or cancel my having been. Mortality does not erase the reality and value of the humanity we are, albeit for a finite time.

That finitude notwithstanding, our interrelated lives affect the ongo-ingness of life; for that reason, my bottom-line value remains that of enhancing the quality of life for all life, whether or not an answerable, humanly satisfactory deity even exists. What I want, then, is to make sure that I have affected other life (both human and nonhuman) in such a way as to enhance the quality of other life. I want to have some way of making the transition from individual being (from my subjective experience) into collective nonbeing (death) with integrity and dignity, and with the love of God, trustworthy in anger and in gratitude, embod-ied in my spouse and in my friends, all of whom will be there for me, both through any suffering I must undergo and at the point of my departure. That is my faith commitment, my personal style of resisting, and my fervent hope. It is also a further indication that my activity of theology as praxis cannot rest, cannot be simplistically content with the dysfunctional nonanswer with which theodicy responds to *both* process and protest theologies.

My first instinct, then, has been that we must move from theodicy to ethics, from obsessive questions about the divine to issues of human responsibility.[41] And yet, I have come to learn the hard way that the very shakiness of our theological and existential grounding precludes a pre-mature or simplistic move in that direction, however ultimately impor-tant that must be. Indeed, I have found myself compelled deeper into the dysfunctional horror in our tradition before I could even begin to discern a way through that darkness into the ethical, life-giving light of day.

Querying the Divine

Whatever provisional resolution I had reached regarding theodicy, whatever tenuous equanimity I had so far achieved in balancing the nonanswer with the ethical demand that resolution seemed to disclose, all my best efforts shattered in mid-decade. Already far too present far too often in our AIDS-ravaged community, the angel of death proved an even more insidious and ubiquitous intruder in our lives during 1995, abusing family, friends, and neighbors alike in ways both symbolically prescient and painfully real.

Before the new year had even begun, my father placed my decreasingly mobile, eighty-nine-year-old grandmother in a nursing home, severing her ties to the only relational ecosystem she had known for over a half-century. My spouse, Bob, and I had just begun to realize the dying process implicit in "our" grandmother's forced relocation, when the young lover of an older gay friend and mentor died of a pervasive cancer which had invaded his already AIDS-ravaged immune system. Fresh from that memorial service, we paid our first visit to Granny in her new residence and were deeply saddened by the obvious decline in her embodied quality of life, a decline hastened at least in part by my father's earlier abuse by neglect and ineptitude. While we were visiting Granny, the oldest of our three dogs died unexpectedly, following some minor skin surgery. No doubt still affected by residues of the anesthetic, her nervous system caused her stomach literally to turn, killing her in the space of some twenty minutes. Only a couple of weeks after burying our beloved (if cantankerous) Abigail beneath a blanket of snow which she would have loved to romp in, we learned that Bob's best friend and the designated executor for his will—a friend whom Bob had just visited the day before—had died suddenly, succumbing to his very first round of AIDS-related *pneumocystis carinii* pneumonia. A return visit to Granny demonstrated to us just how much someone can decline in a mere six weeks. She had lost virtually all remaining independent mobility and become dependent not just on a walker but on wheelchairs and nursing assistance for the simplest and most personal of tasks. At this point, my father put Granny's long-time home on the market, and Bob and I became accomplices in its dismantling. Gradually dispossessing our grandmother meant the slow death of the only constant family home I'd known for over four decades (my immediate family having always been on the move). By Holy Week and Passover, we had grown uncertain whether Granny would even live to her ninetieth birthday in June (she did, although bedridden by then, and she died exactly two months later); an elderly neighbor died from kidney disease and cancer, while another neighbor fell to a sudden and fatal heart attack; and a gay friend had to place his lover in hospice care because of complications from AIDS-related *Kaposi's sarcoma* (he also died within only a few weeks). Although the early summer provided some respite from our engagement with the angel of death, that hiatus proved brief: Granny died in August, and we lost yet another neighbor, this time to AIDS, in September. No sooner had the shofar sounded a new autumnal year, than the young, estranged spouse of a dear friend and colleague finally succumbed to his long battle with AIDS in October; the middle-aged husband of another close colleague died of cancer in November; and another elderly neighbor died in early December. All of this occurred as Bob and I began to worry about the newly discovered changes in our own T-cell numbers and other immune system markers.

So enmeshed was I in the valley of the shadow of death (with ten deaths around us in nearly as many months), it is surely not surprising that my earlier efforts to wrestle with the problem of suffering or the question of theodicy came back to haunt me. I was reminded again that my career as a theologian and the occurrence of AIDS in the gay male community are simultaneous, intertwined from their beginnings.[1] What *was* surprising for me is how conflicts between my father and me over the quality and logistics of Granny's care revived the old abusive dynamics in that relationship. This juxtaposition of parental abuse with suffering and dying is not without theological ramifications.[2] My renewed interest in theodicy, therefore, involves my own experience as a survivor of physical and emotional childhood abuse and, as a gay man, a perennial survivor of society's homophobic abuse. It also reflects my deep concerns for two groups of people who ultimately do not survive: the very elderly and those suffering from the final stages of full-blown AIDS. As I continue to distill and clarify the courage of the everyday, to articulate ways to do more than just survive—in fact to live queerly and defiantly especially when the angel of death is so ubiquitous, so close at hand—I am more and more aware that these issues are not easily separable. Death and suffering, parental and social abuse are all intertwined, and their insidious interrelatedness must be explained as part of the ongoing activities of exploring theodicy and doing theology as a gay man in the age of HIV/AIDS.

• • •

The Divine as Monster

• • •

While helping me revise an earlier manuscript which also addressed theodicy questions, my biblical studies colleague and friend at Agnes Scott College, Tina Pippin, pointedly asked me, "Where is God in the Apocalypse of AIDS?" My immediate answer was an echo of Elie Wiesel:[3] God is the small child hanging on the Nazis' gallows; or, in Tina's tradition, the broken man hanging on the Romans' cross; or, in my experience, the gay man suffering the throes of AIDS. In spite of my publicly professed scripture-phobia, my colleague Tina compels me to keep scripture within the parameters of my theological vision. Likewise now, by reminding me of Job, the force of her question precluded any facile resolution based only on divine empathy. Instead, she disclosed to me the more difficult question lying behind my answer: Is God not also

the Nazi torturer and the one who crucifies—abusing the "only begot-
ten" to death? Is God not also fully embodied in the homophobic gaybasher and in the retrovirus HIV, both of which torture and kill gay
men? In short, is the Divine not somehow both cosuffering companion
and abusing, torturing, horrific monster?

Feeding my scripture-phobia, Roger Schlobin has contended that the
book of Job ultimately reveals that the Divine "is capricious, cruel, and
always beyond human understanding."[4] The Jobian portrayal of a
whimsical, incomprehensible male God who wagers with the (also
male) devil discloses a divine capriciousness that perverts the Divine-
human relationship, transforming the I-thou to an I-it where Job (read,
"all humanity") is the it, a pawn to be played as the object of a wager, an
object of paternal abuse where the abuser is now raised to the level of
divinity itself.[5] We (Job or any of us) are the divinely abused; our very
helplessness, our inability either to understand or to circumvent the
abuse of the "heavenly father," comes to constitute our relationship to
this monster God. We live now in terror, knowing that "the monster can
always come again," to beat us and belittle us as children, to beat us
and kill us as gay adults, to sicken and torture us from within our very
selves as persons living with HIV.[6]

Schlobin also contends that abuse becomes horrific at the point at
which we realize that hope is futile, whether for success and triumph
over the monster god or even simply for escape from its torture. Hope
becomes dread and "this is made darker by the complete absence of . . .
an afterlife," by the implicit assumption in Job and the explicit possibility in my own anti-eschatological theology that "physical death is
final."[7] The dreadful, hopeless darkness ultimately even imperils our
moral capacities: The capriciousness of the Divine and the futility of
hope together shatter moral vision, undermining any ontological
"good"; they violate all our expectations of divine goodness and cosmic
justice, turning meaning upside-down and inside-out and thereby utterly defying our feeble, aggrieved efforts to understand. We are utterly,
terribly, horribly face to face with the nonanswer of theodicy: "In a cosmos completely ruled by chance and wager, divine torment is the game
and good is irrelevant. . . . There is no moral order [and] justice is not
to be found."[8] As the Divine alternately abandons us and capriciously

torments us, like the proverbial cat playing with its prey, theology, theodicy, and ethics crash and burn in the Jobian whirlwind, in the cyclonic admixture of godforsakenness (tragedy) and divine abuse and torment (horror). We are orphaned in the horrific darkness with no possibility of rescue; worse, the *deus ex machina* or rescuing parent/God for whom we long is unmasked as the abusive monster itself.

· · ·

The Divine as Abusive Parent

· · ·

More recently, David Blumenthal has elaborated on the abusive dynamics of Schlobin's monstrous Deity. While it is not surprising that he claims throughout his book that God has "two essential attributes: holiness and personality" (the latter including mutuality and "reciprocal addressability"), what is surprising is his claim that God not only gets angry but also makes mistakes.[9] While I have attempted heretofore to embrace a limited, even sometimes impotent, but nevertheless all-good and all-compassionate God, Blumenthal argues that the Divine is all-powerful but not all-good.[10] The potential for despotism and abuse are horrifically clear. While Blumenthal's conceptualization of God may be unacceptable to many of us, the contributions of the two colleagues that he incorporates into his text help us reckon with the abuse that is implicit in theodicy and often too explicit in our lives.

One of these colleagues is an adult survivor of childhood sexual abuse. She contends that abuse teaches the abused at a very early age to cease expecting comfort, protection, or rescue from those in power, whether parents or God. In fact, she poignantly insists that omnipotence is itself inherently abusive.[11] She also reminds us that while we, Joblike, need someone to hold us in our pain, our anger, even our self-imputed guilt, no one exists to do that but ourselves; if our rescuer is actually our tormentor, we have to deal with our pain and suffering alone, in isolation.[12] More frustrating still, she contends, as adults we learn another painful lesson: Every attempt to confront the abusing parent (or Jobian God) in order to forgive and to effect reconciliation only sets us up for more abuse.[13] The horrific dynamics of abuse persist so into our adult relationships as to preclude complete healing; the shattering of our basic childhood trust—in a benevolent, compassionate, life-affirming parent, Divine, or cosmos—as well as the persistently dysfunctional quality of those relationships well beyond childhood, are so fundamental that trust never can be restored completely.[14]

While to my conscious knowledge I was never subjected to sexual abuse and therefore cannot presume to equate my experience with that of Blumenthal's colleague, her insights compel me to make some very painful connections between the physical and emotional abuse in my own childhood and my later theological development. My father's anger was always out of proportion to events; on occasion he beat me (always with a belt) until his arm grew tired. Needless to say, I do not remember what childhood misdeeds precipitated such inappropriate responses. Far more often, he simply belittled me as bookwormish; sissified; lazy; mechanically inept; and, after my coming out, as unfit for ministry. During my junior high school years he nicknamed me "Priscilla," simply because I had reached an age where I became conscious of my appearance. Ultimately, of course, I found his abuse, both physical and emotional, generalized in the world by class bullies eager to beat up the class sissy, by boards of ministry eager to dismiss gay clergy and search committees eager not to hire gay faculty, and by a society always willing to "beat up a faggot."

The horror of my own hopelessness was redoubled when as an adult I finally realized my mother's complicity in my father's abuse. Although she stood in the doorway and cried when he beat me, she not only failed to intervene (claiming decades later that she, too, was afraid of him then), but she reported my misdeeds to him after his frustrating days at work. Rather than assuming appropriate responsibility for my protection and punishment (in proportion to my misdeeds), she set me up! During my adolescence, she even on occasion adopted my father's nickname for me, as if calling me "Priscilla" was somehow cute.

These themes of abuse have continued to play themselves out in our family. My younger sister was trapped in an autocratic and perhaps physically abusive marriage for over a dozen years, and my younger brother only recently completed a torturous divorce process to escape an emotionally and physically abusive marriage of nearly a decade. Finally, even Granny fell prey to our familial dynamics of abuse: My father's early failure to provide the level of in-home care she needed precipitated an unnecessarily rapid decline that soon necessitated her institutionalization. When Bob and I attempted to intervene on her behalf, my father's old anger reemerged to shout us down, to assert his inviolability and his prerogatives, and to preclude our stepping in. Certainly with parents and family members like these, to conceptualize the Divine as parent in any sense is problematic.

I like to think I am a theologian who has done his men's studies homework. I have learned from James Nelson, for example, that fathers who wound or abuse their sons were themselves wounded by their own fathers.[15] Wounded fathers wounding sons thus becomes a pattern across generations. Part of what we in the currently wounded generation must do to break this pattern is understand how our wounding fathers were themselves wounded and then, even more importantly, astutely and consciously refuse to engage in wounding behaviors toward others. That can be *extremely* difficult whenever we find ourselves on the defensive, our personal cosmos embattled. We must nevertheless undertake that hard work. In my own case, I know my father was wounded early on, even before he was born. His older sister died three months before he was born, stressing Granny in ways that must have stressed my fetal father. My grandfather was a womanizer and a heavy drinker who abandoned his family not long after my father's birth. My grandmother and my father were left alone in an urban environment distant from her rural roots. Granny worked throughout my father's childhood, and although she remarried when he was seven and moved back to her hometown, my kindly step-grandfather never adopted my father legally, presumably for financial reasons.

Knowing my father's history should make it easier. Likewise, knowing that Mother was abandoned by her mother and adopted by an aunt should help me understand that neither of my parents had proper parenting, as I have elaborated elsewhere.[16] While such knowledge does help me to be more reflective about my own behavior, it also complicates my life. Understanding nurtures an urge to forgive, but attempts at reconciliation and full partnership in the family only engender more abuse, particularly from my father. My understanding also complicates how I view my theological development: If an omnipotent father/God is likely to be abusive or tyrannical, one might very well find in feminist thought, as I have attempted to do, some safer, nonpatriarchal alternative. However, if even a gentle, mother/Goddess may on occasion act in complicity with abusive evil, then neither parent is a trustworthy image for the Divine. Surely a truly compassionate Deity must simply be powerless to protect us from suffering or from abuse. In refusing Blumenthal's omnipotent parent/God—both abusing father and complicitous mother—I have been left yet again with only caring divine impotence as I turn to the insights of his second colleague.

A systematic theologian, Blumenthal's second colleague admonishes him (and us) to avoid projecting parental (or social) cruelty, abuse, or sadism upon the Divine. She reminds us not only that it is unhealthy to love and worship our abuser(s), but also that divine love is always the balancing cosmic counterpoint in our tradition to what we experience as cosmic caprice: "However extreme the suffering and the rage . . . a power remains that is understood to be just, to be characterized by steadfast love. . . . The nightmare of brokenness is not absolute."[17] In profeminist language, we learn again to avoid vertically hierarchical and parentally authoritarian conceptions of the Divine and we remember that the horizontal, near-at-hand energy of the web of being seeks the enhancement of the quality of all life, even in the midst of suffering.

The ongoing conversation between Blumenthal and his colleague also raises eschatological questions for me: If one believes in a personal, subjective experience of another life and, indeed, an afterlife with the Divine, would not an afterlife with a capricious, even sometimes malicious, omnipotent Deity actually be more hell than heaven? Conversely, one may take a profeminist and ecologically friendly position, anticipating not a personal subjective experience beyond this embodied interrelational life, but a return to the ever-dynamic, transpersonal energy of the renewing web of being, the very circle of life. Then how can one entrust oneself to that holy circle if the Divinity that comprises it has proven itself capricious and untrustworthy? Blumenthal's sometimes abusive God fails in either eschatology.

Of course, Schlobin warned us earlier that we would find just such ways to avoid reckoning with the monster. Historically our response to utter horror in theology has been avoidance and denial: "The human [recoils] from the non-human, from the void, seeking escape from the truly hideous Other that violates all sanctuaries and sensibilities."[18] Now in trying to avoid facile responses, the actions of refusing to engage or to worship an abusive parent/God and of raising eschatological questions function to distract us, to divert our gaze yet again. We know suffering and death are real, really painful, and tragically ubiquitous. We know horror in our relationships and in our very selves. And yet, if we are to take that horror seriously and neither avoid it nor project it upon the Divine, where and how are we to face the monstrous darkness, look into it, and push through it to some uncertain yet positively transformative theological moment? If madness this way lies, then we must force ourselves, in spite of our maddening fears, to push through that terrifying darkness, that potential insanity, in order to achieve and construct a queer kind of sanity.

■ ■ ■

The Darkness at the Center

■ ■ ■

If Schlobin inverts the traditional mythic warnings, insisting that we look the monster in the eye, and Blumenthal precludes any simplistic abandonment of relationship with the abusive parent/God, then we dare not look away or too easily ignore the power of that relationship in our lives, lest doing so only cause us more grief. In my case, genetics prevents me from looking away; increasingly since turning forty, I face my abuser every time I look in the mirror and I hear his voice in my own. No wonder that since childhood I have internalized my father's scorn, heard his disapproval, overcompensated while awaiting further recriminations or the next blow—living with an all-pervading fear. I am my own worst enemy; I embody both the abusing monster and the terror—perverse God-with-us. Living openly as a gay man for two decades has simply raised this familial abuse and terror to a social level, my openness as much an invitation to perpetual abuse (ecclesiastical, academic, social) as an embodied sign of defiance. Fortunately, this is just the point at which an even more recent writer enters the theodicy dialogue.

Kathleen Sands notes that the "inflowing of the excluded" into the arena of theological activity compels that activity beyond simplistic notions of diversity and inclusivity. Indeed, because "a long procession of the demonized, subjugated, and forgotten is emerging," the reclamation of theological agency by those whom western theology has demonized as "evil" compels theology to rethink the very meaning of evil itself.[19] She later elaborates:

> With the theological emergence of those who have been cast by this tradition as demonic or inferior, "evil" begins to talk back. The Others narrate their own histories of suffering [parental and social] and struggle [social and political], their own memories, desires, outrages . . . [and yet] . . . as the historical victims of injustice identify their enemies and defend themselves, they too are seasoned and defiled by judgments of evil.[20]

Elsewhere she also notes, "Evil is not . . . that which is unintelligible but that which we may understand and refuse; not that which lacks being but the willful destruction or suppression of being."[21] Sands's definition queers "evil," turning "evil" upside-down and inside-out; those who by their acts of abuse willfully destroy or suppress another life, including those they have labeled "evil," are the truly evil. Sands's inverse definition also reveals a deeper problem for the abused: Our experience of ourselves as "evil" gets very confused, to the extent that we have learned—whether by perpetual parental or social abuse in our lives—to refuse ourselves and to act out that refusal by wounding ourselves or others. The resultant inner confusion compels us to (re)consider what it means for those of us who are gay/lesbian, and those of us both parentally and socially abused, to live as the last legalized "other" in a tradition and a society where "other" equals "evil." In short, I must consider what it means for me to see my father in the mirror and to know myself as both evil and good, as pervert and as a theologian.

I am coming to realize that this process by which we gay men have been labeled "other," this process by which I, too, have been labeled "evil," lies at the heart of my own self-acceptance and self-esteem dilemmas. My unwitting internalization of abuse has effectively precluded two decades of progay activism from completely exorcising the self-hatred within. I have tried to speak a resounding "yes" to myself and others, only to be drowned out by the reverberating "no" within. I have tried to articulate and advocate self-acceptance and even liberation theology, while nevertheless falling victim again and again to the abusing parent within—subconsciously naming myself "evil," naming embodied sexuality "evil," naming sexual gay male life "evil." As a result, my every act of defiance—theologically, relationally, sexually—has been accompanied by a heretofore unacknowledged and all-pervading fear of some paternal/divine phallic weapon wreaking punishment upon me. This conflict—my knowledge of myself as both good and evil—along with my fear of parental/divine retribution and my frantic grace-precluding efforts to overcompensate for being "evil" and thereby to avoid certain damnation, altogether constitute the dark center in my life. Indeed, the proverbial heart of darkness is this conflict, this ambiguity, the ambiguity of struggling against all the negative evaluations of my life, my being, and gay being itself—from both without and within—while also trying to discern ways to affirm life, to celebrate my being, and to live ethically as an openly gay man. This ever-present and unavoidable ambiguity requires not only that we assert our goodness while being labeled "evil," but also that we gay men be astute to when and how we are also capable of acting out abuse, of embodying our monstrous parents, in relation to ourselves and others.

The awareness that we must all live with this ambiguity, with the potential for evil always lurking in the darkness at the center of our otherwise good lives, constitutes tragic consciousness for Sands. As already noted, she is painfully aware that we are victimized by evil and yet also "seasoned and defiled" by our own capacities for evil.[22] She argues that for those of us who are parentally and/or homophobically abused, "meaning is a product of a community . . . that is victimized or marginalized. But . . . community [must never be] idealized; it is also the site of

betrayal, loss, and division."[23] We who are gay men are clearly aware of
our losses—to homophobic exclusion, to HIV/AIDS; and to a lesser
degree, we are also aware of our divisiveness, including the absence of
any ethical consensus regarding our sexuality.[24] We may be much less
aware of our capacities to betray and wound ourselves and one another;
we may be unaware just how thoroughly we have internalized our
abusers, both parental and otherwise.

As the all-too-frequent objects of both parental and social abuse, we
gay men must be very careful not to turn our having been and/or our
still being victims of abuse into victimizing and abusing ourselves or
others. As but one example, we must astutely avoid entering into or continuing within relationships with surrogate parent/lovers, relationships
whose dynamics do not heal our wounded self-esteem but only reenact
and perpetuate the patterns of abuse in our lives. Likewise, we
absolutely must not turn our pain and anger into a weapon to hurt others, whether as in-group spitefulness and disdain, as HIV-careless sexual behavior, or as privileged hostility toward other groups (racism, sex-
ism, economic elitism, etc.). Finally, we must avoid futile attempts to
create self-worth through assimilation. Indeed, assimilation to the
abusers' standards is always a trap: When we have so internalized the
negative messages—whether of abusive parents or a homophobic culture—that we no longer resist and defy, then we become accomplices in
our own victimization.

In this sense, any ghettoization, any tacit agreement to live out our
lives where someone else has bracketed them, is a manifestation of our
own complicity in and our acceptance of our set-apartness as "evil," as
"other," as well as our resignation to being targeted for further abuse.
Instead of resigning our lives to abuse, to self-denigration, to homophobia and ghettoization, we must face the terrifying darkness and push
through it. We must say "no" to the "no" always pronounced against our
lives—by wounding parents and gay-baiting society—in order finally to
articulate our "yes." In my case, I must look harder in the mirror, pierc-
ing the parent/monster/God with my gaze to reclaim the good gay son
his image seeks to obliterate. And then, I must go even further: to shift
from passively blaming my father to assertively accepting responsibility
for all the ways in which I have, however unwittingly, become far more
adept at torturing myself than he ever was or ever could be. The monster

in the mirror is not only the judging parent/God, but also the unforgiving and mercilessly punishing self. That is the ultimate monster of monsters I must defeat in order to reclaim not only my good gay self, but indeed my very life. True to the all-permeating ambiguity, my success in this final action/process does not depend solely upon me; it also requires divine companionship and cosmic empowerment to nurture the courage which in turn enables living through and beyond the fears and abuse, from one day to the next. Although such tasks as these are certainly hard work—ongoing challenges, in fact, grounded in ambiguity—we must all defiantly push through our fears to face down the darkness both without and within.

• • •

Tragic-Horrific Theological Method

• • •

As dynamic and dialogical activity, doing theology and ethics increasingly raises more questions than answers, more challenges than solutions; nonetheless, we must make decisions and enact commitments without any answers, without any assurances. It is within this fractured and fragmented web that tragedy inheres. Indeed, for Sands, acknowledging the ambiguity, "the mixture of acceptance and questioning," is a tragic sensibility, a tragic methodology: "Tragedy reemerges . . . because, precisely in the midst of radical plurality, we must make commitments and take sides."[25] She argues that the pluriformity of postmodern life means that our very particularity (as the victims of abuse and/or homophobia, for example) necessarily places us in conflict with other equally valid particularities (e.g., our wounding parents' own woundedness). The inevitability of conflicting ideas and values within that pluriformity lies at the heart of tragic consciousness: Tragedy is inherent in living with conflict and ambiguity as a given.[26]

If Schlobin's monster or Blumenthal's abusive parent/God has undermined any ontological, monolithic good, Sands turns the Bonhoefferian demand to live *etsi deus non daretur* (*as if* God does not exist) into a tragic virtue for pluriform postmodern life: We are called to embrace life with all its conflicts and to make responsible decisions amidst the darkness of ambiguity. To do so is to resist abuse, to act in defiance rather than out of terror, to refuse to be swallowed by the darkness even when the theological ground falls away beneath our feet. In short, it is up to us:

> To feel ourselves unworthy of brutality . . . the power of resistance is nurtured or crushed in the web of relational life. That is how fragile we are; that is what it means to live without metaphysical guarantees. What comes first . . . is not any incorruptible goodness but the dance of life. . . . To abandon faith in a God who protects us from tragedy does involve . . . a real risk of passivity and despair. [But] the risk of drowning in the tragic is not as great as that of clinging to a boat that no longer floats.[27]

Ultimately, neither evil nor good are vertically given. They are horizontal, enmeshed in the embodied relational life of the web of being. To live *etsi deus non daretur* is to engage in "unmooring the good from any metaphysical anchor, so that it becomes an entirely human, entirely fragile creation."[28]

If neither evil nor good are vertically given, neither is justice or injustice. Justice is not some transcendent ideal, but something immanent and fragile, something we must discern and create. As such, justice is clearly not inevitable; it, too, is up to us, dependent upon our capacities to live accountably in relation. While the full realization and implementation of such fragile justice—in this world, here and now—is always a possibility, it is not necessarily a linear project toward which we inexorably improve. Immanent justice eschews the creation-Fall-redemption-eschaton model of linear history. For our ambiguous pluriform reality, there is neither a perfect paradisiacal beginning, nor a cosmically manipulated Fall, nor a single redemptive moment, nor an eschaton to validate (or condemn) our lives. There is just the fragmented reality of our relational and embodied lives—in all their tragedy and all their joy. In other words, we do not need a Deity to make us do the "right thing"; we can discern and enact justice without that theological carrot. Or, in Sands's terms, we can integrate human life and nonhuman life (nature), responsibility and "profound negativity" without reverting to any transcendent supernatural (re)solution.[29]

Granted, the reality of "profound negativity" remains a stumbling block. Tragic consciousness recognizes that utterly unacceptable situations really are true and undeniable; they "cannot be answered by speculation [theodicy] or faith [theology] but only by protest and struggle," by resistance and defiance.[30] In fact, one way to read tragic-horrific theology is that "tragedy is the moral paradox that beings who want goodness [life] cannot remain uncontaminated by evil [suffering and dying]."[31] At the same time, because a horizontal and radically immanent theology such as my own keeps us focused on embodied relational life, the dualism implicit in such a reading—between human evil [horizontal] and so-called natural evil [vertical]—breaks down.

The ongoing struggle with HIV/AIDS in my own life and theology is even now at last capitulating to the breakdown of this dualism. The radical shift in my thinking here has been the dawning awareness that while HIV/AIDS is a "natural" evil, like any other virus, or earthquakes, or the weather, it is extremely difficult to separate it from human acts of responsibility or hatred. Indeed, HIV/AIDS does not happen in isolation but is embedded in complex and overlapping relational webs. In other words, although HIV/AIDS "just happened," we cannot really separate its victims from their social/relational entanglements—either from the ways in which any of us might have contributed to exposing ourselves or others to HIV or, *more importantly*, from the ways in which HIV/AIDS has been and continues to be exploited in multiple occasions of human cruelty and injustice. HIV/AIDS has become the cruelest of ways to label the other as "evil" and thereby to justify blaming the victim. Ultimately, we cannot distill any pure, uncontaminated "natural evil" from HIV/AIDS that is not fundamentally interwoven with these issues.[32]

Just as HIV/AIDS is fundamentally interwoven with human relational justice or cruelty, so also is *being* gay fundamentally interconnected with *how* we are gay. Sands argues that, given the ambiguity of our postmodern lives, "there is nowhere to retreat from the defiling aspects of moral responsibility"; in fact, we must remember and detail our own "defilement" en route to achieving accountability.[33] Those of us who are gay men living in the ambiguity, the mixture, of white male privilege and heterosexist, homophobic abuse, for example, must be aware of the ways in which both parental and social abuse have defiled us, even having been structured into the very dynamics of our own subculture and ghettos. We must not be too quick to look away from our experiences of abuse or victimization. In fact, we should look harder and deeper, not only to understand how we gay men have been and are victims, of abusive parents and/or a homophobic culture, but also to understand how we victimize ourselves and others. Tragically, HIV/AIDS becomes a powerful sign (albeit not the only one) of the extent to which we gay men have been willing to wound one another with our phallic weapons—from protesting bathhouse closings a decade ago, to advocating multiple sexual encounters as the monolithic qualifier of liberated gay identity, to failing to support what too often become undervalued and consequently broken relationships.[34]

Sands further argues that we must do more than "endure and repeat" to achieve something transformative with our lives.[35] We must do more than endure and repeat homophobic exclusion by life bracketed in our ghettos and their bar-based, late-night, sexual subculture. We must do more than replicate parental abuse in hurtful relationships and/or in perpetually low self-esteem. Tragically again, our contentment simply to endure and to repeat is why even HIV/AIDS—all that it has taught us about grief, mortality, compassion, and caregiving notwithstanding—has not fundamentally reshaped our ghettoized lives and sexuality.[36] To live transformatively instead, to acknowledge and yet defy tragedy, we must also defy our enemies by loving ourselves enough to refuse to embody parental/social abuse in self-denigration or in relation, as well as to refuse any definition or ghettoization by heterosexist constructions transposed upon us and accepted by us. Regardless of the nature or the source of the abuse and victimization we experience, we cannot succumb passively to that abuse or to our fears of further retributive abuse. We cannot get stuck in a futile search for something or someone to blame for our lives—not a God, not an abusive parent, not our homophobic culture, not even ourselves. Instead, we have to assume appropriate responsibility, not for the abusive past imposed upon us, but for our lives in the present and immediate future. *We have to be responsible for our own lives.* This, rather obviously then, is finally the point at which we can undertake the movement from theodicy to ethics, certain that we have faced the darkness and that, having done so, we are indeed ready to move through it and beyond it.

$\mathcal{D}$oing Gay Ethics

In spite of the very real possibilities of horror and tragedy in the world as we know it, our lives matter. In spite of—in fact, because of—our mortality, our bodies matter.[1] Gay and lesbian bodies matter. Bodies living with HIV and AIDS matter. A truly liberating ethics will begin with and among these bodies that matter, with and among our bodyselves in relation to other bodyselves. In fact, as I have argued elsewhere, everything we know, everything we feel, and everything we experience—including our experience of relation with self and others, with nature and God—all these things we know and experience through and only through our relational embodiment.[2] Among those colleagues who share this fundamental epistemological starting point with me, Sallie McFague has pointedly noted, for example, that "the body is not a discardable garment cloaking the real self" because the real self *is* the mortal, embodied person—a bodyself.[3] Likewise, Beverly Wildung Harrison has elaborated on the epistemological and ethical aspects of our bodyselves as the very loci of our being:

> All our knowledge, including our moral knowledge, is body-mediated knowledge. All knowledge is rooted in our sensuality. We know and value the world, if we know and value it, through our ability to touch, to hear, to see. *Perception* is foundational to *conception*. . . . All power, including intellectual power, is rooted in feeling. . . . If we are not perceptive in discerning our feelings, or if we do not know what we feel, we cannot be effective moral agents. . . .

[Moreover], our capacity for caring, for expressing and receiving deep feeling, for reaching out to others is grounded in and through our bodies.[4]

Echoing Harrison, whose work she edited, Carol Robb further argues that valuing our embodiment means "attending to our bodies as sources of moral data and the foundation of our moral power."[5] More adamant still on this point, James Nelson argues not only that our embodiment as sexual beings is foundational to our capacities to feel and to enact compassion, but also that our sexual embodiment is actually a prerequisite for our even being moral creatures: "Moral knowledge . . . is bodily: If we cannot somehow feel in the gut the meanings of justice and injustice, of hope and hopelessness, those terms remain abstract and unreal."[6]

To radically (re)value our bodyselves in such a fashion will entail a number of activities: In seeking to discern ethical ways of being with/in the world, we need to celebrate ourselves as sexual bodies and we need to honor the full spectra of sexual orientations, expressions, and communications; we need to value and to enact mutuality in relation; we need to eschew gender roles and other stereotypical and confining ways of acting, for ourselves and for others; and, we need to trust the heretofore subjugated knowledge and the moral wisdom of the oppressed.[7]

For those of us who are gay men and lesbians, giving full credence to the subjugated knowledge in our bodyselves means recognizing both that it is *in our bodies* that we know and experience the horrors of marginalization and that this embodied experience is the primary standpoint or criterion for our ethically critical and prophetic analyses. As bodies we bear the cost of familial rejection. As bodies we carry the burden of professional, academic, and ecclesiastical exclusion. As bodies we feel the blows, the bruises, the aches and pains of antigay/antilesbian violence. And in our bodies we grieve for and remember those whose bodyselves have been taken from our midst by AIDS. I experience the life and dying and death of my friends and loved ones in and through my body, not in or through theirs. Even my empathy for their suffering bodyselves is something I only know in/through my bodyself. Revaluing my bodyself and their bodyselves and, together, our embodied web of relationships—revaluing the body in solidarity with other bodies—also means that the inevitable death of my subjective, experiencing bodyself does not obviate my responsibility for other bodies, for their quality of life, and for their future. Indeed, ethics and justice begin with ourselves, our bodyselves, by "befriending ourselves—loving our bodies" and *by treating ourselves and one another well.*[8]

. . .

Right Relation and Resistance

. . .

Clearly, starting with our bodyselves is not a starting place in isolation from others. For the activity of ethics, beginning with our bodies necessarily entails beginning with our bodies in relation, as Robb reminds us when she insists that the "personal autonomy" of the ethical bodyself "in no way involves a solitary or disengaged self."[9] Instead, ethics is relational and contextual, grounded in empathy and responsibility—for our bodyselves, for other bodyselves, and for the relational web we constitute together. Focusing on concrete bodyselves in relation rather than on ethical abstracts—thinking contextually, relationally, and interpersonally—calls into serious question the very concept of ethical objectivity. Ethics is not some static "object," not some set of universal rules that enjoys ontological status apart from human bodyselves in relation, not some set of rules to which we should or even *could* all conform. Indeed, "rather than thinking of [ethical] situations as primarily dilemmas or crises during which one must deliberate and choose" (as if we could do so "objectively" apart from the web of relations in which we find ourselves embedded), we must instead come to understand doing ethics "as a way of being in relation with other life . . . [as] the larger field of interaction that constitutes shared life."[10] Not an object, doing ethics is an activity, a way of being with/in the world. Similarly, values are neither ontologically "given" nor handed down from the Divine; values are created by human choices.[11] As but one example in feminist and gay theologies, the concept or value of justice is not to be understood as some putatively objective, rule-based notion of fairness, but is to be understood as something dynamic and contextual—as right relation.

What emerges in the activity of "doing ethics" is an "alternative" objectivity that draws upon flexible, frequently unrepeatable, and "often distinctive situations and relationships" rather than upon putatively repeatable, universal, impartial, and impersonal detachment.[12] As an activity of bodyselves in relation, an ethics not of detachment but of engagement develops and nurtures a social objectivity by pooling, hearing, respecting, and being transformed by the broadest possible spectrum of difference, by the very richness of our diversity. Says Robb, "objectivity itself is a social product that results when we put forward our perspectives, are self-assertive, hear the perspectives of self-assertive others, [and] allow ourselves to be challenged and changed."[13] Here at last we find an alternative to heteropatriarchal concepts of objectivity: An "alternative" understanding of objectivity does not require emotional disinterestedness; nor does it seek or desire human homogeneity. As a result, an "alternative" objectivity does not preclude advocacy of the oppressed; rather, it challenges every idea and practice that oppresses, exploits, or excludes women, gay men and lesbians, other oppressed persons, or the earth itself. Such an emergent alternative objectivity and its related ethics-as-activity are inclusive of all life. Recognizing that "nothing that is of us can be alien to our theology,"[14] our alternatively objective ethics "depends as much on restructuring our senses of moral responsibility in intimate partnerships, sexual relations, communities of personal loyalty, and day-to-day work relations as it clearly does on replacing institutional, legal, and political arrangements."[15] Our alternatively objective ethics-as-activity, an activity shared by bodyselves in relation, is an inclusive both/and that dynamically fuses the personal and the political.

Bridging the personal and the political in the tasks of liberation ideally means developing a broader, more inclusive vision that sees the connections among all forms of oppression, exploitation, and disvaluation and thereby facilitates liaisons to confront all of these. Not through co-optation, but through cooperation—by working together to achieve liberation for all peoples and for the earth itself, for example—will gay men and lesbians find our own liberation achieved as well.[16] To do this, our alternatively objective ethical activity must nurture solidarity while it also respects and honors diversity. One mark of solidarity is our willingness to be both vulnerable and accountable. Says Harrison, "Solidarity is accountability, and accountability means being vulnerable"; she further suggests that our shared stories constitute the vulnerable self-disclosures which facilitate both accountability and solidarity.[17] As we share our stories, our vulnerable self-disclosures, we see more clearly both our differences and our points of commonalty. We come to realize that genuine solidarity—real inclusiveness—does not mean melting-pot sameness which blends away difference into some bland, homogeneous, lowest-common-denominator consensus. Rather, it does mean that both our intellectual work (theory) and our actions (praxis) must enhance difference and learn from it; we must embody both respect and empathy for other embodied locations of oppression that are different from our own. Sharon Welch has captured well the both/and of solidarity/diversity when she writes that "solidarity has two aspects . . . (1) granting each group sufficient respect to listen to their ideas and to be challenged by them and (2) recognizing that the lives of the various groups are so intertwined that each is accountable to the other."[18]

Our ethical activity will indeed insist on the value of, and the accountability in, diversity. All too often, however, we have feared diversity and difference as harbingers of chaos. Although there is of course nothing "inherently problematic or wrong" with difference or diversity, we have nonetheless looked upon "pluralism and complexity as problems to be solved rather than [as] constitutive elements of social organization"; in doing so, we have failed to realize that "differences can be a source of richness, insight, and variety" which enhance the quality of our shared lives as bodyselves in relation.[19] Rather than understanding difference either as indicative of inequality and hierarchically higher or lower value, or as a rationale for domination, exploitation, and exclusion, our diversity can be "understood as richness of possibility" as we learn to "live with complexity."[20] Indeed, "the problem is not diversity but how we approach differences and the power, privilege, and prejudice that our culture has structured around it. . . . Differences will divide us as long as they are the basis upon which any group is denied power and resources."[21]

Revaluing diversity clearly challenges any hierarchical power and privilege imbalance. The long-cherished heteropatriarchal equation that "sameness equals good equals control" ultimately discloses that whenever the standard for equality is a white, Christian, middle-class, Euro-American, heterosexual male, equality is only achievable insofar as (or to whatever degree that) one is capable of approaching that standard. Gay men and lesbians, along with all other life forms excluded from this standard by definition, have increasingly realized that "when individuals who are not white and male [and heterosexual] demand that their differences receive the same attention as do those of [heterosexual] white males, this is denounced as asking for special treatment."[22] Our demands as gay men and lesbians for the same civil rights protections as those begrudgingly extended to other minorities in this country, for example, are far too often and far too easily dismissed as just such pleas for "special rights." Rather than uncritically endorsing the controlling value of sameness by apologetic efforts to assimilate into mainstream culture, we must push beyond the quest for equal rights and protections—however important to achieve they still are—to an advocacy and a celebration of difference which goes well beyond whatever the letter of the law might be. We must realize with Welch that a "foundational ethical critique" actually *requires* difference, that "the creation of a moral vision and a strategy of moral action requires . . . the counterbalance of other groups and individuals."[23] We are reminded by her insights that "the chaos of interdependence can be viewed as itself positive, as the fertile matrix of human creativity, leading to richer political and intellectual constructions as the [partial and perspectival] insights and needs of various groups are fully taken into account."[24]

Our chaotic and fertile interdependence is yet another indication that we are bodyselves in relation. Insofar as doing ethics is a relational activity and not a static, "abstract, authoritarian, impersonal, universalist view of moral consciousness," our lives as diverse ethical beings in solidarity with one another greatly depend upon our embodied capacities for mutuality and compassion.[25] Because we know that "relationality is

at the heart of all things" and that "we are part of a web of life so intri-
cate as to be beyond our comprehension [and] part of a vast cosmic
web," our ethics must embody a mutuality and a reciprocity which brook
no hierarchy and which insist upon utter equality.[26] Such radically equal
mutuality and reciprocity is more commonly understood as love. Harrison has eloquently described the power of "love in its deepest radicality"
as well as the consequences of our failures to embody such love:

> We have the power through acts of love or lovelessness literally to create
> one another. . . . Because we do not understand love as the power to act-
> each-other-into-well-being we also do not understand the depth of our
> power to thwart life and to maim each other. . . .
>
> It is within the power of human love to build up dignity and self-
> respect in each other or to tear each other down. We are better at the lat-
> ter than the former. . . .
>
> The love we need and want is deeply mutual love, love that has both
> the quality of a gift received and the quality of a gift given, [not] the cloy-
> ing inequality of one partner active and one partner passive.[27]

Particularly as we contemplate the meaning of love and discern how
to embody that love during the AIDS health crisis, we must indeed
guard against "cloying inequality." We must learn that there is no hierarchical value assigned either to the one who gives care or to the one
who receives care. Indeed, the "real pleasure of mutual vulnerability"
lies in the experience of both "truly being cared for" and "actively caring
for another."[28] Our radical mutuality, embodied in our capacity for
compassion, further strengthens our solidarity in the midst of suffering.
As we act out our compassion in relations of mutuality and reciprocity,
we also embody God-with-us, as Welch describes:

> The power of compassion is divine . . . expressed in simple acts of
> acknowledging each others' fear and pain, . . . caring for a friend dying of
> AIDS, acknowledging, without diminishment, the pain that others feel;
> the power of saying "Your pain is real, your cries are heard, your anger is
> just." . . . This power of compassion and anger is holy.
>
> Resilient connections with other people and the earth bring joy, pain,
> and wisdom. [They] are the presence of grace.[29]

Equally important during a health crisis that requires so much compassion and caregiving is a vital caveat that further underscores the
value of mutuality and equality, or reciprocity. The hard lesson
bequeathed to us by women's experience and feminist insights is that
solidarity, including solidarity with those who are suffering and even
dying, is absolutely *not* to be understood as a call for self-sacrifice or an
invitation to guilt. Solidarity includes our present mutuality and
accountability as bodyselves in relation; it does not include either our
self-denigrating guilt or our survivors' guilt. Similarly, it entails an
"enlargement of the self to include community with others" and not the
self-diminution that results from sacrificial self-denial. As Welch noted
earlier, "The love that heals is far from . . . self-sacrifice. It is founded in
love of oneself, a difficult task for those who are judged less rational,
reliable, and honorable than white middle- and upper-class [heterosex-
ual] men."30

This is a difficult task, indeed, because far too many of us do battle
daily with our demons of low self-esteem. Specifically for gay men and
lesbians, these demons are nurtured by homophobic disvaluation and
exclusion, by antigay/antilesbian violence, and by the ways we too often
incorporate these negative messages into the daily construction of our
very being. As we learn to purge our bodyselves of internalized homophobia, as we learn to embrace our gay/lesbian lives in spite of our
demons of low self-esteem, and as we (re)construct our lives as
assertive, unapologetic, self-affirming bodyselves in relation, we also
come to realize that our choices to care for one another are not matters
of self-sacrifice. Whether in our day-to-day relations generally, or
specifically in those relations shaped by HIV/AIDS, we come to realize
with Sarah Hoagland that our choices actually constitute who we are:

> That we have to make choices is not a matter of sacrifice. . . .
>
> We can regard our choosing to interact as part of how we engage in liv-
> ing. Such choices are a matter of focus, not sacrifice, . . . part of how I cre-
> ate value. Far from sacrificing myself, or part of myself, I am creating. . . .
>
> In acting, engaging, making choices, we are creating something. We
> create relationship, we create value. . . . We create . . . meaning. . . .
>
> If we regard choice as creation not sacrifice, we can regard our ability

to make choices as a source of enabling power rather than as a source of sacrifice or compromise.[31]

Not our propensities for self-denial and sacrifice, but our creative power to make choices that sustain mutuality, reciprocity, responsibility, and caring enables God in our midst. Our self-affirmation in the face of homophobia and our caregiving and care receiving in the midst of HIV/AIDS are also actions of resistance. And, as Ron Long has reminded us, to choose to enact resistance and hope is to embody the Divine, to empower the divine energies in our midst which in turn empower us.[32] Indeed, our ethical activity as bodyselves in relation is not only marked by our efforts to celebrate diversity and to nurture solidarity in the tasks of liberation; it is also informed by how we experience and create resistance to all those structures and forces arrayed against us.

Resistance is an extremely significant leitmotif in both gay and feminist theologies. Gay/lesbian activists, for example, can be seen as constituting overlapping communities of queer resistance, collectively embodying the divine resistance so important to Long's doctrine of the Divine. Among feminist theologians, Welch has most thoroughly elucidated the implications of resistance for theological ethics, noting early on that "joy in the abundance of life enables and motivates resistance to the exploitation and destruction that vanquishes the possibility of such joy."[33] An embodied theological ethics recognizes that we know joy and resistance as well as the "vanquishment" of that joy in our bodyselves: In our bodies we know marginalization and victimization, and in our bodies we must also move beyond passive victimization to active resistance. In our bodies we must come to understand "the intricacies and fluidity of the power relations that victimize women and many men," such as gay men and men of color, even if coming to that embodied understanding also implicates "many of these individuals [ourselves!] in victimization of others and of themselves."[34] In short, understanding resistance entails our also reckoning with marginalization or victimization as we know it, in our bodyselves, both as our experience of oppression and as our capacities to oppress others.

Whenever we fail to deal adequately with our experience of marginalization or victimization, whenever we too quickly put aside that aspect of our embodied identity, these occasions constitute actions of putting the proverbial cart before the horse. They are intellectual or political leaps which threaten to undercut our most genuine and most inclusive resistance. The current trend among some gay/lesbian academics to eschew identifying with victimization, for example, comes prematurely, failing to examine or take seriously enough both the continuing power and the debilitating effects of an as yet homophobically constructed culture on our embodied lives as gay/lesbian people and/or as people living with HIV/AIDS. Too many white gay men cannot even agree as to *whether* we are oppressed; neither have we achieved much, if any, consensus regarding an analysis of the structures and meaning of continuing antigay/antilesbian oppression and violence in the 1990s.[35] No doubt, those gay men and lesbians who have achieved safe and comfortable places in the academy, in the churches and synagogues, and in the larger economic value system so idolatrously worshiped in the West are trapped by their very complacency. Those white gay men and lesbians who believe themselves tidily assimilated, who further believe our only difference is what we do in bed, have not only forfeited a fuller understanding of what being gay or lesbian means but, worse, have also forfeited their responsibilities to examine their own positions of racial and socioeconomic privilege vis-à-vis other oppressed persons and the earth itself. Welch pointedly reminds us that the costs of such compromised privilege and complacency include cynicism and despair in regard to the possibilities of any more thorough or more inclusive liberation than the meager tidbits with which many of us have contented ourselves to date:

> The temptation to cynicism and despair when problems are seen as intransigent is a temptation that takes a particular form for the middle class. . . . It is a despair cushioned by privilege and grounded in privilege. It is easier to give up on long-term social change when one is comfortable in the present. . . .
>
> It masks the bad faith of abandoning social justice work for others when one is already the beneficiary of partial social change.[36]

Rather than too quickly assuming assimilationist comfort in privileged and putatively unoppressed positions, we must first understand our oppression and our marginalization, we must realistically confront the horrors in our lives. In order both to know ourselves and to know our bodyselves in relation to other oppressed lives, we must confront these horrors before we can, in turn, move beyond reductionist identities as victims. Of course, we want to avoid being "just victims." However, if we are serious about grounding gay theology and ethics in embodied, lived experience, then we have to face the ways in which that experience is shaped by homophobia—a homophobia that is itself embodied in and by our society, by many professions, by the churches and synagogues, and even by many of our families. We must realize the importance both of "discovering how to learn from pain [from oppression] without trying to conquer it or to become immune to it" and of recognizing that "although there is a way through, there is no way out"; in other words, it is healthy to be angry and to grieve the fruits of homophobia, to experience pain and learn from it, to neither trivialize nor cling to suffering or defeat, and then, and only then, to know when and how to move on, to be able to risk oneself again in the tasks of liberation.[37] Clearly, victimization per se, victimization as our only identity, is inimical to our lives as bodyselves in relation. A reductionist clinging to one's role as victim only perpetuates that role: It fosters the myth that gay men and lesbians are easy targets for exclusion or physical violence. It reinforces the closet; together our assimilation to mainstream society and our acceptance of the status quo become disempowering second closets. It becomes an excuse for not taking responsibility, sexually and relationally, and thereby for sanctioning failed relationships and lapses from safer sex practices as if we do not "deserve" any better. Likewise, it also becomes an excuse for not taking responsibility for the ways in which we exploit and oppress the earth itself, other persons, one another, and even ourselves. And it allows us to avoid understanding the complexities of power and to avoid discerning alternatives to the heterosexist "power over" to which we have forfeited our lives, as nothing more than victims.[38] In short, to accept an identity as "only" a victim signals

capitulation to the horrors in our lives; at the same time, to deny all victimization and to pretend the horrors are not there only makes us more
vulnerable to them. The point is that we must neither minimize the
meanings and costs of marginalization nor allow ourselves to be reduced
to only victims—another both/and for our theology. We must defiantly
and queerly understand what it means to suffer and *to rejoice* for being
gay or lesbian, while refusing to be passive victims, whether of
antigay/antilesbian violence, homophobic exclusion, HIV/AIDS, or even
our own subculture(s) and sexual underworld. While we must not ignore
or stifle our pain or our righteous anger at injustice, we must also celebrate our strengths, our victories, and even our partial successes.

Much like our experience of some degree of safety and comfortable
privilege, any expectation of "quick fixes" and easy solutions also threatens to undermine our resistance against persistent and deeply
entrenched structural dynamics. Welch comments, "The inability to
persist in resistance when problems are seen in their full magnitude . . .
is of critical significance."[39] Indeed, I suspect that one reason why
some gay men and lesbians are hurriedly moving to reject any sense of
identity based on victimization or marginalization is because they are
suffering from "battle fatigue," from the sheer fatigue of battling anti-
gay/antilesbian oppression writ large for a quarter-century (at least),
coupled with the perception that we have made too little progress.
Unlike the 1970s, when white gay men (among others) assumed that
our liberation would come easily, politically on the heels of the civil
rights and other movements of the 1960s—unlike those heady days
before Anita Bryant's 1977 antigay/antilesbian campaign and the even
more disillusioning politics of AIDS in the 1980s—the 1990s and
beyond confront us with hard, eye-opening reality. There will be no easy
answers, no quick fixes. Or, as the late Michael Callen observed,
"Homophobia is firmly, firmly entrenched. I believe this generation [of
gay men] has been raised to expect instant success because so much
progress was [apparently] made so quickly [in the decade before AIDS].
. . . A severe backlash [is] waiting in the wings."[40]

If we are to avoid succumbing to horrific despair and if we are to
have the queer strength necessary for dealing with backlash and recur-
ring obstacles to our liberation, then we must be prepared for a long-

term struggle, a struggle likely to persist well beyond our present generation. Welch convincingly argues that "maturity is gained through the recognition that evil is deep seated, and that the barriers to fairness will not be removed easily . . . , that work for justice is not incidental to one's life but is an essential aspect of affirming the delight and wonder of being alive"; indeed, that "the horizon of action is recognition that we cannot imagine how we will win. Acknowledgment of the immensity of the challenge is [now] a given."[41] The challenge is not to forgo understanding the embodied meanings of gay/lesbian marginalization or to mask the realities of oppression with the compromised complacency of quasi-assimilation; the real challenge is to claim and to celebrate our courage and our tenacity as people who will not just go away.

Although we cannot and will not resolve all the problems of homophobia and heterosexism in our lifetimes, we can provide "a heritage of resistance" for those gay men and lesbians who are even now coming after us.[42] We can accept the hard fact, for example, that the generation of us who most clearly remember and annually celebrate the birth of the modern gay/lesbian liberation movement during the Stonewall Inn riots of 1969 may profit little from any changes forthcoming from our sociopolitical and theological efforts. We are not likely to be invited back into ordination or into full membership in the academy on our own liberated terms. We *are* likely to find that our position on the margins is our home for life. At the same time, we can rejoice in the likelihood that we do create greater possibilities for those who are coming after us. This likelihood, this redemptive possibility, is a sign of the creative freedom available to us at the margins and, as such, is one antidote for despair, for half-hearted acquiescence to the status quo, and for assimilationist complacency. It opens up the further possibility of a long-term vision that can renew our embodied resistance and (re)empower our lives as bodyselves in relation.

Such a life-giving vision will also more fully appreciate and value those momentary, even fleeting liberational actions—those small or partial successes—that nourish us and sustain us. As these small successes accumulate in our collective lives as bodyselves in relation, we learn that "where there is . . . oppression, there is also, always, a history of survival and resistance to oppression that needs to be recalled and celebrated for the marks of dignity, courage, and potential it bears"; after all, "even failed resistance bears powerful evidence of human dignity and courage that informs our contemporary vocations."[43] For example, as gay/lesbian pride celebrations in the 1990s have begun to change from primarily political rallies to celebrations of our lives as gay men and lesbians, we have begun to take more seriously the importance of our history of resistance. Recalling even our smallest victories among larger defeats—our "memories of defeat and memories of defiance"—sustains our liberational efforts in the face of persistent opposition; our "dangerous memories" inform our collective "sense of dignity [and] they inspire and empower us" to continue to challenge oppression on every front.[44]

Our "dangerous memories" keep us connected to the circle of life by also keeping us unrelentingly aware that no matter how difficult, or even at times seemingly impossible, the larger goals of liberation may appear—for gay men and lesbians, for other oppressed persons, and for the exploited earth itself—those goals are still worthy of our commitments and our actions. As we celebrate our small victories along the way, we learn (again) that although our experience of marginalization is constitutive of who we are, we are not just victims; our embodied lives in relation are even now making a difference, enhancing the quality of all life. As we remember the defeats and the partially successful defiance disclosed by our history of resistance, we learn (again) how to maintain our self-respect and how to choose our battles ever more carefully. While increasingly "strategic" risk taking will not create any ultimate, final, or total success, it will create "the conditions necessary for peace and justice" and thereby increase our chances for future successes.[45] As we learn (again) that assimilation can ultimately lead to the death of our imaginations and our capacities to care, we also learn to discern the fine line between an "accommodation necessary for survival" and a "creative defiance," which only together can further enhance our lives and further empower our increasingly savvy liberational efforts.[46] By wise and responsible actions in community, we come to know (again) in our bodies the wisdom of Welch's insights, both "the recognition that we cannot guarantee decisive changes in the near future or even in our lifetime [and] the equally vital recognition that to stop resisting, even when success is unimaginable, is to die."[47]

Because "silence equals death," we dare not stop resisting. An increasingly savvy resistance that walks the fine line between enhanced survival skills and "creative defiance" also teaches us the importance of our righteous anger, our loving actions, and our mutual power with one another. While anger may be one legitimate and humane response to the dilemmas of theodicy, anger frozen, anger directed at the Divine without prompting us to action, risks degenerating into an impotence far more damaging to our embodied human lives in relation than even so-called divine impotence before suffering and evil. Instead, anger directed at righting wrong relation, at creating justice as right relation, here and now, becomes liberating, transformative anger. Harrison has wrestled astutely with both kinds of anger, ultimately advocating that anger which, shared and nurtured by the Divine, is tantamount to love:

> Anger is not the opposite of love. . . . Anger is a mode of connectedness to others and it is always a vivid form of caring. . . . Anger is—and it always is—a sign of some resistance in ourselves to the moral quality of the social relations in which we are immersed. . . .
>
> Where anger rises, there the energy to act is present. . . .
>
> Where feeling is evaded, where anger is hidden or goes unattended, masking itself, there the power of love, the power to act, to deepen relation, atrophies and dies.[48]

Anger repressed, forced inward, undermines self-esteem and demoralizes us. And yet, anger shouted vertically heavenward in protest or declared vertically downward in judgment does little more to facilitate corrective action. Only horizontal anger, dynamically transformative in the "social relations in which we are immersed," is such a resistant and "vivid form of caring" that it becomes embodied as love in action. After all, neither anger nor love is primarily about our feelings per se. Loving feelings are not ends in themselves. Empowered by our righteous anger at injustice, we act our way into feeling, we embody love in action: "Moral quality is a property of acts, not feelings, and our feelings arise in action. The moral question is not 'what do I feel?' but rather 'what do I do with what I feel?'"[49]

As we shift our understanding of anger from the vertical to the horizontal, from individual feeling states to actions in relation, we also find ourselves moving further away from an understanding of power as vertical (power-over) to power as horizontal and shared (power-with). Much like transformative anger, power-with can be—must be—proactive and empowering, creative and resistant, never inwardly directed or passive (powerless). Our power in relation, our power-with, is the generative product of our deep and mutual caring, another way of understanding that energy of collective resistance that literally keeps us going—in the face of oppression, of AIDS, even of the smaller day-to-day problems with which we regularly strive.

A horizontal power-with that facilitates our very survival finds it fullest embodiment in friendship: "It is because of deeply rooted friendships that we are able to sustain the energy necessary to make substantive social change in an often unfriendly world. Ideology alone is simply not a sufficient motivator when times get tough. But acting because of and with friends is a powerful, sustaining force."[50] Rediscovering the resistant power of friendship, reclaiming the survival-enhancing strength of embodied right relation, brings us full circle. Moreover, if we are serious about valuing and treasuring our friendships as sacred locations of dynamic right relation and resistance, then we owe it to ourselves and to our friends to undertake a careful articulation of the ethical "how" of our lives. Such an exploration cannot help but further enhance the quality of our lives, shared together as friends in community.

* * *

Phenomenology and Prophecy

* * *

As she delineates her particular feminist theology of friendship, Mary Hunt interjects an important caveat: "As lesbian/gay relationships are increasingly visible and accepted, a major issue is what ethical norms will guide such relationships. . . . It is not enough to say that all is now permissible where nothing used to be allowed. . . . Neither is it fair . . . to leave everyone with the impression that there are no lesbian and gay sexual ethical parameters."[51] To discover and to name oneself as a gay man or lesbian may well be to take a giant step out from (or to find oneself brusquely pushed from) the mainstream, patriarchal, and heterosexist culture wherein traditional moral discourse inheres. "Traditional morality," whatever that means, is probably simultaneously an ethical framework we reject in coming out as gay/lesbian as well as a moral realm that rejects us. Our movement to the margins, however, should in no way be construed as the discovery of a place where "anything goes."

To claim and to live out one's gay/lesbian being as a mode of being with/in the world is not to live in an ethical vacuum. Sociopolitically, for example, it is not enough only to demand justice for *what* we are—for being gay or lesbian; we must also take responsibility for what we do—for *how* we have been and for *how* we are—as gay men and lesbians. Or, as Harrison succinctly puts it, "*Do-ing* must be as fundamental as *be-ing* in our theologies."[52] In short, doing theology and doing ethics conflate. Unfortunately, this reflective movement from "what" to "how" has been slow to emerge in the gay/lesbian communities. Gay men at least have only just begun to undertake this important ethical work. Sadly, we are far from consensus—even polarized—in our approaches to the ethical question of "how?"

In addition to my own voice raised earlier to explore and appraise gay sexuality,[53] two other, very powerful voices on these issues have recently emerged from within the gay male subculture or "ghetto." They are the voices of Ron Long and Michael Callen. While both men speak from similar, commonly held urban gay experience, their passionately different, even polarized, conclusions about gay male sexuality not only demand our attention, but require me and all of us together to (re)establish and nurture a dialogical exploration of how we might best construct our lives as gay men.

The first of these two outspoken men, my friend and colleague Ron Long, is never shy about declaring what he believes essential to being a gay man. Long makes gay male sexual desire and its fulfillment central to an understanding of gay male identity. He places gay male sexuality and its primary context, the bar-based urban gay ghetto, dead center in his own theological work. He contends that "gay sex is a way for two . . . gay men to come to know and feel themselves to be men"—to know themselves to be masculine—and that, therefore, "sexual engagement is a way of experiencing the self as impressively, masculinely male. . . . Tricking facilitates the achievement and sustenance of a masculine identity."[54]

Tricking, or engaging with numerous and often anonymous sexual partners, is a highly valued gay male experience for Long. He is deeply concerned that our theology not disvalue or dismiss our one-night stands. In fact, he argues that multiple sexual encounters outside the parameters of relational intimacy need not be dehumanizing experiences of sexual objectification. (However, he concedes not only that gay men in the sexual hunt are reduced to their lowest common denominators—denigrating intellectual, career, or other individualizing markers irrelevant to the purely sexual arena—but also that neither partner in such an encounter is "really interested in the historical density of the other as [a] full individual."[55] Long's insistence on a phenomenological or descriptive approach to gay male sexuality, an approach that adamantly refuses to critique gay behavior, further discloses the dynamics of such encounters: "The other person is, for the moment, not an individual who is appreciated in the fullness of his individuality, but is rather a 'concrete universal.' . . . Tricking is . . . an interaction whereby each [partner] comes into touch with his own masculine maleness through the mediation of a representative male other."[56]

Reappropriating "masculine maleness" for gay identity is the other hallmark or highly valued experience in Long's sexual theology. Gay male identity and spirituality are tied inherently to sexual desire and its fulfillment in the genital encounter of any two "impressively, masculinely male" gay men, according to this view.[57] Nor is Long apparently troubled by the potential elitism and sexual reductionism implicit in his thinking. He concedes, for example, that "if sexual interest is responsiveness to [masculine] beauty, then it's inescapable that there will be a privileged elite." He risks reducing gay masculinity to frequent male genital experience when he concludes, "To sense the self as cock is to be empowered as a man in the world. . . . The cock is the sign, symbol, and . . . vehicle of masculine identity and empowerment."[58] The temple for such phallic worship is "the sexual delivery system of the bars," which are so frequently the central foci of the urban gay ghetto. That Long values not only masculinely genital sex, but also the "sexual delivery system" of the gay ghetto and the ubiquitous bars that make such sex possible is unabashedly clear when he further insists that "gay theology is more powerful to the degree that it can own the ghetto as home."[59] Long's sexual theology and its nonjudgmental, phenomenological relationship to gay male sexuality is most assuredly at home in, and in fact already embodied by, the gay male ghetto which he so openly and passionately embraces.

Long's insistence that we honor the positive, liberating, and life-enhancing aspects of the gay ghetto in our theology is clearly important. The ghetto, including the "sexual delivery system of the bars," provides a necessary oasis of safe space in the midst of a homophobic and often violently antigay/antilesbian culture. At the same time, as Hunt has already reminded us, our safe space must not be anything-goes space. As one of the major voices in the emerging dialogues that constitute gay men's theological work, Long is certainly to be praised for bringing not just eroticism but sexuality itself back into the gay theological arena. His body theology celebrates our sexual bodyselves and does not mince words in describing what that has been like in his experience. We clearly need such a sexual phenomenology in balance with descriptions of our marginalization in order for us to have the most complete understanding possible of our total experience as gay men—particularly if we intend to employ that experience as a primary resource for our theological activity.

Long's particular phenomenology fails, however, precisely because of its putative objectivity and its adamant refusal to be critically or prophetically reflective on the experience(s) it discerns. Long's rather voyeuristic phenomenology risks doing more harm than good; by refusing to be critical, his putative objectivity in fact functions to sanction and encourage a particular gay male status quo which permeates gay male life and keeps too many gay men locked into a purely sexual understanding of that life.[60] If so-called objectivity is merely a ruse to maintain privileged power structures in place—changing nothing and liberating no one—then Long's phenomenology likewise provides no liberational vision for growth or change. That lack of vision may be clearest in Long's acceptance of a heterosexistly reduced understanding of gay being and gay sexuality. Not only does he embrace traditional Western concepts of masculinity as preferable for gay men, but he goes on to make multiple sexual contacts normative for those "impressively, masculinely" gay men. He uncritically worships the phallic symbol of heteropatriarchal power-over in an elitist display of dominance and privilege over anyone not masculine or sexually active enough to meet this norm. His implicit misogyny reinforces the heteropatriarchal masculine status quo—simply transposed into a gay context—without envisioning a new, more liberating masculinity for gay men or for men in general. Simply adding receptivity or penetrability to the standard list of accepted masculine attributes in not enough.[61]

Unfortunately, Long's implicit misogyny is not the only point of elitism or exclusion in his theology. Not only does he essentially concede that only handsome, masculine men are qualified to meet his phenomenological norm for gay identity, but, in putting the white gay male ghetto of New York City at the center of his observations, he also risks reinforcing the invisibility of gay, lesbian, bisexual, and transgendered people of color within the larger gay/lesbian community(ies). This exclusion further oppresses persons already treated as invisible in their native ethnic communities and continues to foster misogyny, racism, and economic elitism among urbanized white gay men. It continues to nurture the wrong-headed idea that both homosexuality and homophobia are somehow only "white issues." In addition to its exclusionary power, such an uncritical endorsement of the white, urban, gay male ghetto only reflects our failures to subvert the hegemonic heterosexism that consigned us there in the first place and our own willingness to live out our lives in spatial and temporal territories defined or constructed for us by that hegemonic, homophobic culture. Whatever its value as safe space may be, therefore, to place the white gay male ghetto on a pedestal as normative for gay life not only fails to liberate those white gay men themselves, but also excludes all those other persons who do not fit this "new" norm. What we need instead is to be very careful not to conflate the rich diversity of gay/lesbian identities and modes of being.

The dangers of exclusion and overconflation also plague the spirituality that emerges from Long's phenomenology. Not only does he conflate gay masculinity with gay genital sexuality, he also reduces gay spirituality to gay sexuality. His body theology goes too far. Moreover, like his idealization of the ghetto, his idealization of his own sexual experience as normative for gay spirituality again risks excluding anyone who does not enjoy or participate in the kind of sexual life he celebrates. In short, Long makes not only the white gay male ghetto, but his own individual sexual experience as well, normative for gay identity and gay spirituality.[62] Such a myopic perspective cannot see how frequently our culturally constructed masculine socialization processes have produced men and gay men who are incapable of or dysfunctional within intimacy—how many gay men, for example, too easily substitute multiple sexual encounters for the intimacy missing in their lives. He cannot see that, while tricking may occasionally result in a redemptive moment for both participants, it just as easily becomes an obsessive and addictive behavior which precludes intimacy and avoids relationship. His phenomenology fails to realize the extent to which every gay male ego in this scenario becomes the center of its own universe. It fails to recognize the anonymous sexual encounter he idealizes as a self-centered moment wherein the other person is clearly means (object) and not end in himself (subject). This implies that we are simply to exploit one another to satisfy our own selfish sexual desires and, in that process, to masculinize ourselves—to shore up an assimilationist gay version of heteromasculinity nonetheless still called into question by heterosexism.[63] In other words, in his painstaking effort to honor the tricking moment in his theology, he has failed to honor the tricking partners themselves, as full subjective human beings.

Overall, then, while Long's phenomenological approach to gay sexuality and thereby to gay sexual theology succeeds in bringing fully embodied sexuality back into the center of our theological conversations, it fails insofar as it simply reinforces sexual reductionism, sexual objectification, and white gay male elitism. It does not help us affirm human difference beyond what we do in bed; nor does it help foster mutuality in relation or diversity in community. Rather than creating vision, it narrows our vision, falsely suggesting a monolithic understanding of what it means to live as a gay man. A truly liberating gay theology and spirituality can surely provide us with a better ethical foundation than this. Indeed, Long's phenomenology provides us with no criteria whatsoever for ethically constructing either our sexuality or our lives themselves. Without such criteria, we are unable to gain an ethical perspective on our lives from his work.

What we need instead is both a phenomenology of gay experience— a description of our lives which celebrates the full, rich diversity of our many varied lives and which reckons with the limitations and obstacles to those lives—and an empathetic, compassionate, even critical perspective for enabling and enhancing the fullest quality of life for all of us. In short, we need both phenomenology and prophecy in our theology to keep us accountable both to ourselves and to others.[64]

• • •

Prophecy and Accountability

• • •

Through all the varied voices that nurture my own voice and clarify my own ethical perspective on gay life, one leitmotif emerges over and over again—accountability. Indeed, accountability in relation is the absolute value or criterion we need for appraising all our ethical work. Accountability is both requirement and by-product of our friendships, of our diverse bodyselves in relation. We develop our accountability in and through these embodied relations both in order to know how we oppress one another and in order to know how to advocate on our own and others' behalf. Accountability is interwoven with our vulnerability, our willingness to be transformed and to grow. It is a sign of our interdependence, our cooperation, our friendship, our solidarity. Our accountability is our love in action, befriending ourselves, one another, our community(ies), our earth. It is the embodied ethical posture that enables us to create meaning, to create choices, and to choose life— even in the face of AIDS. It also enables us to be more than passive victims, to develop and embody resistance, and to weave a legacy of resistance for the long-term, multigenerational tasks of liberation. And, because our accountability is part of a relational dynamic—at once vulnerable, transformative, and liberatingly resistant—it necessarily opens us to loving, life-giving self-criticism.

As early as 1972 Rosemary Radford Ruether cautioned her feminist colleagues against championing the oppressed-who-can-do-no-wrong.[65] Gay men and lesbians must be equally astute, neither wallowing in our victimization nor elevating our embodied ghettoization or marginalization to some inviolable—and thereby utterly ineffectual—pedestal. The descriptive work of phenomenology and the critical work of prophecy must go hand in hand, balancing each other, because neither self-sacrifice nor self-worship will do. What we must deal with instead is a red herring too common in the gay/lesbian community(ies): Loving self-criticism, prophetic words both from and to our own embodied lives in relation, are absolutely *not* symptoms of unresolved, internalized self-hatred or homophobia. Denigration of our gay/lesbian siblings may be; defensive refusals to hear and consider criticisms may be; but prophecy lovingly tendered is not. Nor is self-criticism a symptom of despair; it is rather an antidote to such privileged, middle-class enculturation. Indeed, "the ability to be self-critical, to remain open in a systematic structural manner to revision, is a sign of maturity." Moreover, "the work of revision and self-critique is grounded in strength, not weakness," and not self-hatred.[66]

To approach loving maturity rather than self-hatred, our prophetic word to our own community(ies) must be qualified by empathy, by love and compassion, by solidarity and empathy, by an acknowledgment of our own complicity in ways of being gay (or lesbian) which have been inimical to appropriate self- and other-love and which therefore have not only hampered our liberational efforts but have also placed our very lives in jeopardy.[67] As we engage in prophetic self-criticism, our ethical reflections must also acknowledge the possibility (and, insofar as possible, guard against the likelihood) that those reflections will be co-opted by those who stand arrayed against us and even inverted/perverted to fuel condemnation of our very lives.[68]

As but one example, while we gay men need to claim transformative responsibility for our past (and present) sexual behavior, that active wrestling-through must in no way be interpreted or exploited so as to "blame the victims" of AIDS! Indeed, we must adamantly insist that the

mandate of compassion in our tradition should not be understood dual-
istically and thereby only tendered to the presumed innocent while
denied to the presumed guilty. Just as Carter Heyward has insisted that
our society owes justice and the "basic conditions of human worth to *all*
people," regardless of sexual orientation,[69] so, too, compassion is due to
all persons living with HIV/AIDS. Whether one is responsible and/or
accountable for having exposed him/herself to HIV (through even one
occasion of unprotected sex or needle sharing) or whether one is totally
without responsibility for his/her HIV status (such as most hemophili-
acs and all infected infants), how the need for compassion arose is irrelevant to the demands of compassion. Says pastoral theologian Earl
Shelp, "Enabling, sustaining, and enriching [care] should be offered in
obedience to the love command to all people regardless of a [person's]
moral evaluation of the behaviors that contributed to the creation of
need"; in short, "a person's need and that alone is sufficient to require
. . . a loving response."[70] The mandate of compassion does not elevate
any of us to the position of judge; we are not called to judge addictive
behaviors or sexual behaviors or in any other way to engage in "blaming
the victim." Instead, as Shelp has also reminded us, we need to develop
more complete understandings of the total dynamics involved in intra-
venous drug use and the other high-risk behaviors that can expose an
individual to HIV.[71]

Indeed, specifically for gay men, our turn toward loving and non-
blaming self-criticism actually begins not with finger-pointing at ourselves or at other individuals, but with a (re)examination of the cultural
context in which we find ourselves. Harrison explains, for example, that
because heteropatriarchal culture has constructed the meanings of
masculinity only negatively—as not-woman, as not-effeminate, as not-
homosexual—the resultant, culturally embedded homophobia "incorporates and encompasses all of the power dynamics of misogyny." It
specifically has bequeathed to us stereotypes that all homosexual males
have failed to be masculine; that all homosexuals are sexually receptive
pseudo-females; and that all oppressed men, just by virtue of their not
being in power-over, are effeminate.[72] Rather than engaging in a naive
and unreflective idealization of gay male misogyny and masculinity,
such as that implicit in Long's sexual theology, it behooves us gay men

instead to revisit certain aspects of our own cultural context, specifically the western masculine socialization process, which we have all had to deal with to some degree or other. I even suspect that many of the problems affecting gay men and our relationships result not because we are gay but because we are socialized as men.[73]

One way to break the vicious cycle(s) of masculine socialization in our embodied gay male lives is to confront the fears veiled by that process. Foremost among these fears are our culturally maintained fear of intimacy and the related fear of any mutuality wherein we might lose control. In the decade prior to AIDS, for example, a portion of the gay male subculture institutionalized certain patterns of behavior that prevented both healthy confrontation with these fears and any possibility of intimacy. As a result, the emerging pre-AIDS sexual subculture often precluded intimacy and reduced many of its human participants to merely genital machines. By severing ourselves from our sexuality, our masculine socialization precluded too many of us from any deeper erotic pleasure than fleeting accumulations of genital experience. In our bodyselves we learned to ignore whole-bodied eroticism by distancing our "selves" from our "mere genital functions." At the same time, our socialized male need to control led us to manipulate our minds and bodies with drugs and alcohol in order to make ourselves perfectly tuned sexual machines. We learned to compensate for the stereotypes around effeminacy and receptivity with extremes of behavior, both as "tops" enacting hypermasculinity and refusing ever to be penetrated and as "bottoms" forcing our alienated bodies to receive ever larger items. We overcompensated for our perceived failed masculinity by sexual prowess, sexual performance, and sexual achievement. We allowed our entire self-worth to become tied to our "impressively, masculinely" sexual attractiveness, while at the same time we became ever more alienated from our bodies as ourselves. As a result, for many of us, the heyday of discos and bathhouses was every bit as exhausting as it was exhilarating.

What we have failed to see in all of this is the degree to which heterosexism in the years following World War II actually set us up. The bar and bath subculture, for example, kept (and the bars still keep) far too many gay men safely one-dimensional (i.e., only sexual). It keeps us hidden away in the dark, late hours where the heterosexual world, which does not want to see or even to acknowledge us anyway, has tacitly agreed to bracket us. If being gay has been defined for us by heterosexism as only being sexual, we have turned sex into an art form and an industry. In short, we have accepted and embodied the very stereotype of promiscuously sexual, only and always sexual, homosexual males that heterosexism constructed for us.

Prior to AIDS, the gay sexual subculture in collusion with masculine socialization taught us to separate sex from love or friendship, consequently leaving many of us with lots of sex, but few if any deeply satisfying and mutual relationships. Some of us even competed with our lovers for sexual conquests outside our primary relationships. Early gay male political discourse simply mirrored these myopic self-understandings as it defended our "right to love"—a thinly veiled phrase for actually defending our freedom of access to sexual license. Only as we grew weary of the endless rounds of the sexual netherworld and, later, as we encountered AIDS invading our sexual domain, did we gradually come to realize Hunt's warnings regarding lives where "anything goes." Only gradually did we surface from an underworld delimited by heterosexist parameters to realize that what we really need is not more sex but more love, love in committed relationships and in friendships based on justice as right relation, regardless of whether anything genitally sexual is involved.

One writer who did surface, and the second of the two outspoken men whose voices emerge from the ghetto to address our current ethical endeavors, is Michael Callen. Callen is also perhaps the best known long-term AIDS survivor, finally succumbing in late 1993 after twelve years of full-blown AIDS. The tragedy is that Callen's voice has been not only largely ignored, but viciously attacked. The red herring of self-hatred, the heterosexist reductionism of gay men to only sex, and our own socialized acceptance of that definition and our resultant need for continued sexual freedom at all costs hardened our hearts. During Callen's life, portions of the gay male community had already begun to assault the messenger in order to ignore the message.[74] It is ironic that Long's sexual theology (which never acknowledges HIV/AIDS or preventative safer sex practices) emerged concurrently with Callen's AIDS death and yet anachronistically celebrates an idealized view of the very gay male ghetto and gay sexual practices that Callen himself criticized. A polarized tension thus remains between the ghettoized life Long applauds and the alternative life Callen longed for. To better understand this tension, which continues to haunt our efforts to construct ethically sound lives as gay men, we finally must listen to what Callen said. Indeed, because this man who was so adamantly antireligious articulated so clearly some of the content appropriate to an ethics of sexual accountability, we must look more closely and listen more carefully to what he so compassionately tried to teach us.

Callen was tenderly and passionately committed to enhancing both the quality and the longevity of life for his fellow gay men, even as he spoke critically to us. He was, for example, painfully aware of the costs of the closet of heterosexism, both personally and historically, noting that "prior to the gay liberation movement, gay people looked in the mirror of American culture and never—not once—saw our image accurately reflected. . . . The only information . . . said that all gay men are promiscuous."[75] He bemoaned our collective failure of imagination, our inability or our unwillingness to construct alternative definitions of what being gay men could mean. He was saddened by the tyranny of collective belief that not being sexually free enough somehow meant not being adequately or sufficiently gay and that, as a result, "we thought of our bodies as [sexual] machines" and we infused our politics with just such myopic vision. "One strain of seventies gay liberationist rhetoric proclaimed that sex was inherently liberating; . . . it seemed to follow that *more* sex was *more* liberating. . . . [In fact] being gay *meant* having lots of sex."[76] In an interview a week before his death, Callen elaborated on this portrait of an early gay male subculture trapped in its own too narrow self-understandings:

> By age thirty-two the average gay man with AIDS has had 1,150 different sexual partners. This was at the peak of the disco era and . . . drug use. . . . [By the late 1970s] there was a new rule . . . that what being gay was about was purely sexual . . . and [gay men] built institutions—sexual playgrounds—without thinking through the long-term consequences of what might happen. . . .

It never occurred to anybody that the cumulative effect of all this par-
tying could be greater than the sum of its parts.[77]

In other words, Callen was passionately concerned not only that we
have so narrowly understood liberation in sexual terms, but also that we
have been so naive. Accepting mere sexual freedom as the sole meaning
of our liberation not only shortchanged our embodied lives, forfeiting
the deeper multidimensional richness of gay being, but also opened our
bodyselves to a plethora of diseases. While some writers in this period
actually counseled us to take pride in our accumulated sexually transmitted diseases (STDs), Callen argued that these diseases were necessarily taking their toll on our bodies, making us ripe for something that
could not be cured easily by antibiotics: "This level of sexual activity
resulted in concurrent epidemics of syphilis, gonorrhea, hepatitis, ame-
biasis, venereal warts and, we discovered too late, other pathogens."[78]

Although it is terribly painful for some of us to share his eye-opening
vision, Callen rightly perceived not only that heterosexism, homophobia, and masculine socialization set us up for narrow self-concepts and
ultimately even for AIDS, but also that we collaborated with great aban-
don in our oppression and in our retroviral near-genocide. We helped
set ourselves up by our own complicity, our willingness to accept heterosexist constructs of what it means to be a gay man—that being gay is
one-dimensional, totally focused on sex. Equally damaging was the
extent to which the most visible and audible portions of the 1970s and
early 1980s gay liberation movement also focused on sex, on the freedom to be utterly sexual, to be just as promiscuous, albeit now openly
so, as our homophobic culture had always accused us of being anyway.
Finally, of course, a sex-negative culture in collusion with a gay sexually reactionary politics made us ripe for AIDS. Even if promiscuity is not
simplistically read as the sole cause of AIDS (as the multifactoral,
cumulative weakening of our immune systems from STDs before we
were ever exposed to HIV), at the very least the gay subculture's obsession with sex orchestrated the conditions by which we made ourselves
vulnerable to any number of diseases and may very well have helped to
spread HIV faster among certain portions of our community. Callen
was simply dismayed by the continuing naiveté of our leaders in the

face of these possibilities, noting that by the early 1980s "gay leadership seemed paralyzed by the mind-boggling prospect that unforeseen consequences of the sexual freedoms we'd fought so hard for might now be killing us."[79]

Because Callen did care so unrelentingly for life, his own and others', he continued to place his subcultural self-critique in sociopolitical context. He was aware both of the dilemmas presented by the very concept of gay community and of the fears and uncertainties AIDS generates. He was equally aware that together these factors affected our participation in the medical politics of AIDS. He observed that in the often fractious gay/lesbian community(ies) as well as in the larger, even more fractious society, "we spend more time fighting each other than we have spent fighting for the true cause[s] and treatments" needed for AIDS and we neglect perhaps truly wise alternative proposals because they do not come with the "right" scientific credentials or governmental endorsement. He argued further that these dilemmas persist because "AIDS is a disease that requires the daily management of massive amounts of uncertainty, and people cling to any certainty they can find. Even if it's false."[80] He was particularly concerned that this overwhelming need for certainty, the overwhelming urge for easy answers and quick fixes, encouraged both gay men and society at large to focus too quickly upon a single cause of AIDS (the HIV retrovirus) and a single primary treatment protocol (Retrovir or AZT).

Given the vagaries of the disease syndrome's manifestation and/or progression in different individuals, given the equally variable toxicity of AZT in those same bodyselves, and given the gay male community's own early ambivalent relationship to safer sex practices, Callen was not only skeptical that HIV alone is the sole cause of AIDS or that AZT alone is the appropriate or best treatment. (AZT has since proven more effective and less toxic in smaller doses in combination with newer drugs, such as ddi, ddc, d4t, 3tc, etc., approved by the FDA after Callen's death.) He was also concerned that the apparently simple one-cause/one-treatment approach to AIDS would only further undercut an ethical perspective on our lives and our behavioral decisions. He argued that easy answers and quick fixes undermine our accountability: "The single-virus theory . . . took away all responsibility from the victim. You just happened to have had an unlucky [sexual encounter]. It didn't have anything to do with the . . . sexually transmitted diseases you had and all the drugs and staying up late and the abuse that you did to your body."[81] The odds of the unlucky sexual encounter, like those of winning a state lottery, made it very easy to accept the politically correct (read, "not threatening to sexual freedom") admonitions of the early to mid-1980s merely to limit and to know one's sexual partners—a certain "recipe for death."[82] Our misperception of those odds also made it that much less imperative for those of us firmly established in our sexual proclivities to retrain ourselves for the differentness and assertiveness required to ensure safer sex techniques. Those purported odds turned too many of us into gamblers who then refused to take appropriate (neither self-blaming nor self-denigrating) responsibility when we did in fact turn up HIV-positive. We had played our lottery tickets and won a lottery whose ultimate grand prize could very well be our deaths.

Callen astutely reminded us, of course, that the alternative to irresponsible gambling or to equally irresponsible self-pity and victim-blaming (including blaming ourselves) is accountability. As our theological ethics also attempts to do, he walked the fine line between accepting responsibility for contributing to the conditions of risk—accepting responsibility for behaving in ways that could expose us to HIV—and being either self-blaming or guilt-ridden because of that exposure. Ever the balancer, he encouraged all of us to move more realistically and more responsibly forward, to see in AIDS "a challenge to *finally* begin living fully" and not just to begin dying.[83] .

Taking responsibility, acknowledging the ways in which we set ourselves up for exposure to HIV, while also being critical of the ways in which our heterosexist and homophobic culture also set us up, is an important both/and for our ethical lives. To accept the hard truth about the way in which many of us lived in the not-so-distant past and about how we allowed ourselves to be exposed to HIV, and then to take responsibility for how we live from now on, is to embody accountability. To take responsibility is most assuredly not to engage in self-hatred; taking responsibility is healing and life-giving. Accountability *is* resistance to AIDS and AIDS death. Callen knew this well; he observed that long-term survivors take "responsibility for their own healing . . . to acknowledge some personal responsibility for life-style choices, both in terms of getting sick . . . and in terms of getting well [but also being] quick to carefully distinguish the notion of taking responsibility for getting well from the counterproductive attitude of blaming oneself for being sick."[84] In his living, his long-term survival, and his dying, Callen also taught us the art of forgiveness—especially to forgive ourselves rather than to deny the realities of our lives. Compassionate self-criticism is an embodied act of love, not hatred. If complicity and silence equal death, accountability surely equals life.

■ ■ ■

Accountability in Relation and Gay Ethics

■ ■ ■

A critical perspective such as Callen's can help us to see our sexual past and our frequently AIDS-permeated present in fresh ways that make possible a future for us all. We can understand AIDS in our community, for example, as one catalyst among others for a shift from a narrow ethics of uninhibited sexual freedom to an ethics of caring for one another, including caring for the "casualties," at least in part, of the consequences of that sexual freedom. We also realize in this process that our ethics cannot simply sanction and authenticate every gay/lesbian life-style or every aspect of the gay ghetto; instead it must move beyond phenomenology alone to provide and nurture a genuinely liberating vision.[85]

As we begin to articulate such a vision, doing gay/lesbian ethics will necessarily be connected to the real embodied lives of gay men and lesbians and to our experiences of continuing to live in a heterosexist and homophobic society. Rather than focusing on victimization or ghettoization alone, however, our efforts will address how we experience both marginalization and empowerment. As our understandings of what it means to live ethically as gay men in particular have shifted from an emphasis on access to sexual freedom to the complexity of justice-seeking and the tasks of AIDS-related caregiving, our commitments to oppose homophobia and heterosexism have broadened to advocate solidarity with other people and the earth itself and to eliminate double standards in every arena of life.[86] Treating gay/lesbian experience with both respect and critical perspective enables us not only to address "local" issues such as sexuality and exclusion, but also to appreciate and work on behalf of "global" issues such as racism, classism, militarism, and environmentalism.[87]

Beginning to make these connections and to facilitate solidarity entails both celebrating our own diversity and that of others and allowing ourselves to be enriched, even transformed, by that diversity, as well as joining in common cause against those forces and structures that oppress any life. Our developing ethics must insist on such solidarity— as both diversity and common cause—particularly with women and the earth, as well as across racial lines and other categories that separate and exclude. We must learn to see and to value diversity as intrinsically valuable, without in any way hierarchizing difference such that it becomes an excuse for inequality. For example, if being gay or lesbian is eventually found to be largely biogenetic, we must be at the forefront of insisting that does not mean gay/lesbian being is any lesser form of life than any other; we must insist that difference does not imply or require inequality.[88]

Such a critical perspective also helps us see more clearly still what at least some of the real moral issues are: We already know by now that the real moral issue is not that some people *are* gay or lesbian but *how* we are living as gay men and lesbians. Likewise, the real moral issue is not about AIDS as a punishment for homosexual behavior; an ethical response to AIDS focuses instead upon the acts of omission and commission that have ignored and/or blamed the victim and in so doing have allowed so many to suffer and die. More specifically still, the real moral issue is not about where, how, or with whom (or even with how many people or how often) we put our genitals; the real issue is the quality (life-enhancing vs. dehumanizing) of the relationships with ourselves and those with whom we share sexually. True to his own life story, Callen agreed with Long to a certain extent, conceding that "promiscuity has its place" in gay male culture, while immediately going on to add that "the point is, whatever sex one chooses to engage in . . . it should be safer sex and . . . it should proceed from a loving instinct to communicate with another human being, rather than being about merely scratching a physical itch, with no regard for the humanity of the individual [one is] scratching the itch with."[89]

Callen's comment brings us back once again to Hunt's concern that we discern some parameters for gay/lesbian sexuality and echoes Harrison's insights that "sexual communication, at its best, mutually enhances self-respect and valuation of the other" and that "sexual touch opens the way to other dimensions of human intimacy."[90] Revaluing our sexuality, not as something restrictive, addictive, or compulsive, but as that active embodied engagement of our erotic energies which enhances our relationships and nurtures our shared quests for justice as right relation, is a significant ethical task for all of us—one already elegantly elaborated by such feminists and profeminist men's studies scholars as Carter Heyward and James Nelson.[91]

Worth reiterating here is that elucidating ethical parameters for our sexuality need not result in a simplistic or moralistic endorsement of monogamy or so-called heterosexual mimesis, as if monogamy were somehow sacred in its own right. Indeed, a decision to frame our sexual behavior within the context of a monogamous relationship is purely pragmatic, neither divinely given nor carved in stone. A decision to be nonmonogamous simply presents a number of thornier ethical questions: Not only are we confronted with the difficulty of maintaining the special, even sacramental, aspects of our primary sexual and emotional relationships in balance with our outside sexual partners; now we must also ponder how *not* to make those encounters alienating and objectifying, on the one hand, and how *not* to exclude our partners or threaten our primary relationships if our outside encounters do develop humanizing friendships. Whether, or to what extent, such a balancing act can be maintained over time clearly remains an open question.[92]

What is ultimately far more important than the issue of monogamy or nonmonogamy is the value of fidelity. All too often monogamy does not include fidelity in its broadest sense, and only empty relationships endure in such instances. At the same time, fidelity includes far more than simple monogamy. It entails much that is not particularly sexual at all, such as honoring and not abusing the feelings of the partners. It includes not only listening well, but also speaking honestly, from our depths—to be vulnerable rather than to hide what we feel. It means "we must be real with one another, really present."[93] We must also be faithful to our values within our relationships; we must cherish openness and honesty and we must trust one another deeply; we must be committed not only to our individual growth as persons but also to the growth of our relationships themselves. Hence, we must be willing to struggle together, to forgive and to heal one another, and to move together into the future. We must indeed be "at home" with one another, sharing all the multidimensionality of our relationships as the sure foundation, the one "place" where we know fundamentally that we belong and that we belong together.[94] Monogamy then becomes not simply a restriction on genital behavior or a form of heterosexual mimesis, but rather a pragmatic and mutually chosen means for nurturing the healthiest and most holistic sexuality in relation for two people committed to a common process of growth and liberation together. With this broadened understanding of fidelity, we can find in Heyward's words the liberational insights we need for our journeys as sexual beings in relation:

> We may decide to be sexually active in relation to only one person . . . because we believe that this is our best means of taking care of the relationship with a person we have come to love in a primary and special way.
>
> The decision to be monogamous . . . may be an honest way of embodying and sustaining fidelity to the relationship. . . .
>
> [It] may be our least emotionally confusing way of building and sustaining trust in a particular relationship as the locus of what is, for us, an extraordinary, uncommon experience of erotic power as the love of God.[95]

We also find, not surprisingly, that what Heyward describes as fidelity sounds a lot like what Hunt describes as friendship. Genuine friendship embodies fidelity. Hunt in fact argues both that "all friendships include a sexual dimension, however implicit it may be" and that, conversely, "sexual relations are usually most satisfying when carried out between close friends."[96] Sexual expression can lift a friendship to a qualitatively different place, while friendship in turn enhances that sex-

ual encounter. Once again we are reminded that quality is more important than quantity: The mutuality and depth of caring intimacy inherent in friendship (a special I-thou relation) enables us to know and to
embody a sexuality far more satisfying than any quantity of anonymous
or objectified (I-it) relations ever could. In short, our ethical reflections
have come full circle once again, as we rediscover the importance of
friendship, not only as the erotically and dynamically embodied location
of right relation and resistance in our collective lives, but indeed as *the*
key umbrella concept or ethical value that can serve, not as an "objective" rule, but as *the* broad guideline for developing our ethically
responsible and embodied lives as mature gay men and lesbians in relation to one another, other persons, and all other life. After all, accountability in relation *is* friendship!

Although the gay monastic St. Aelred of Rievaulx (1110–1167 C.E.)
provided certain long-overlooked insights and guidelines for friendships
in a same-gendered, albeit sexless context,[97] more recent efforts have
been slow to emerge. Kath Weston has enabled us to understand how
friendships contribute to our extended and our constructed, chosen
families, while Hunt has specifically focused on friendship as valuable
in and of itself.[98] Hunt's elucidation of the qualities and aspects of
friendship draw on much that we have already discovered. Friendships
are embodied, not restricted to sex but frequently including it, because
"every relational act is a physical event"; in fact, our friendships can
enable us to celebrate pleasure, including sexual pleasure, "within the
parameters of responsible relating."[99] Friendships also embody power-
with, in the mutuality and reciprocity of an equal give and take. Here
Hunt echoes Harrison who reminds us that "genuine equality . . . must
mean equal dignity in relation and in power."[100] And of course, as we
already know, mutuality of caring and power-with is another way to
understand relationally embodied love which, in friendship, is a "commitment to deepen in unity without losing the uniqueness of the individuals."[101] Such love accepts the embodied beloved, nurtures appropriate self-love, and nourishes a generativity well beyond the heterosexist reductionism of generativity to only that of "making babies."[102] Loving and generative friendship is also voluntary and intentional, paying
attention to and intending the well-being of the other, of one's own

bodyself, and of the collective body in which we find ourselves immersed. For same-gendered friends, friendship is thus both erotically empowered and most generatively embodied in shared justice-seeking action.[103] Justice and accountability are primary characteristics of our friendships because our closest relationships are the contexts in which we first learn and want to learn how to be responsible. Within the mutual support of friendships, we learn how to embody justice as right relation and how to be accountable to ourselves; to our friend(s); to other gay men and lesbians; to other oppressed persons; and even to the full, biodiverse, ecosystemic earth itself.[104]

Because she writes as a lesbian as well as a feminist theologian, and because she is aware that not only the urge for justice but also the power of the erotic informs friendships, Hunt is also painfully aware of how homophobia has shaped and often thwarted same-gender friendships. Culturally embedded homophobia negatively affects same-gendered affection. For example, it prevents men from developing deeply intimate and/or physically affectionate friendships; and, for gay men in particular, it thwarts even appropriate self-love: "If one cannot love another person who is like oneself, it is very hard to develop the kind of ego strength necessary for healthy self-love."[105] Conversely, of course, Hunt argues that we must learn to befriend our bodyselves, one another, and the pluriformity of all life.[106] Just as homophobia often thwarts the possibility of friendship among persons of the same gender, so its correlate, heterosexism, imposes on us a relational standard—marriage—which both disvalues friendships and totally excludes same-gendered commitments. Our heterosexist cultural mindset does not treat any nonheterosexually married friendships as if they matter; mainstream Christianity, ironically, continues to criticize so-called gay promiscuity while refusing to sacramentalize or support gay/lesbian coupled commitments.[107] More frustrating still, in our efforts to dismantle homophobia and heterosexism generally and to displace the marriage standard specifically as the only model for acceptable relationships, far too much "politically correct" gay/lesbian rhetoric has also failed to value gay/lesbian couples as embodied models of friendship. We must not be too quick to dismiss gay/lesbian couples (or couples in general) as if they are by definition not capable of embodying loving friendship as well as romantic love. To do so is to do ourselves a grave injustice.

The accusation that gay/lesbian couples are merely imitating heterosexual marriage (heterosexual mimesis) is another dangerous red herring; it is a disempowering and unsupportive bit of illogic of which even Hunt is guilty. While she at first encourages us to celebrate all our relationships in order to "mark their stages and to encourage their deepening," she too quickly moves to devalue the importance of monogamous or "closed" gay/lesbian couples, based on the argument that they are nothing more than imitative, patriarchal dyads.[108] Granted, couples must be wary of isolating themselves by their own early infatuation, remembering instead to nurture and be nurtured by their other friendships—those relationships that constitute constructed family and community.[109] Nonetheless, all gay/lesbian coupling need not and actually does not represent an assimilationist desire or effort to imitate heterosexist and homophobic patterns. Indeed, gay and lesbian couples (and our constructed family networks, as well) can themselves be sociopolitical units of collectively embodied resistance, at once constituent members of the larger gay/lesbian community of resistance and household units of resistance interspersed throughout the wider landscape outside the gay ghetto. Gay couples can be resistant and activist while also being deeply loving and committed embodiments of fidelity and long-term companionship at their fullest and best. Gay/lesbian coupling and activism constitute a both/and, not an either/or as Hunt and others have contended.

If by virtue of being the same gender in our couplings we can also avoid the pitfalls of heterosexist gender roles, our egalitarian relationships might not only embody friendship at its best but also prove the model really worthy of imitation *by heterosexuals*. Indeed, especially for a people whose relationships are almost universally discounted and our very ability to enter into and sustain loving relationships denied in many narrowly moralistic quarters, we need to lift up and celebrate healthy long-term couples—not as imitations but as models of depth, friendship and mutuality, and freedom from gender roles. (Re)valuing coupling is particularly important for gay men, whose same-gender friendships have been disvalued by homophobia.[110] As we have already seen, our homophobic cultural mindset has made it easier for too many gay men to engage in objectified, depersonalized, and dehumanized genital sex (frequently and with many different men as sex objects) than to engage in friendship or to sustain a long-term relationship. Whenever two gay men can learn to overcome these impediments to intimacy and depth in relation—impediments that are part of the legacy of masculine socialization in our society—we have cause to celebrate their commitments rather than to dismiss them merely as examples of heterosexual mimesis.

Overall, then, as we (re)learn to value both our committed relationships and our friendships, to befriend our gay/lesbian bodyselves in relation, and to demand that we be valued alongside all other equally valuable life on earth, we can also become prophetic embodiments creating a future—a future beyond the ghetto and beyond AIDS, a future beginning right here, right now. We can realize, for example, that couples, single men and women, friendships between couples and singles, and various other configurations of friendships are all equally valuable and equally important constituents of community. We can also remember that quality, not quantity, of friendships is what truly enhances both our individual embodied lives and our collective body; that "security in equality" is only possible in our most mutual relationships; and, that our best friendships, our healthiest long-term relationships of whatever configuration, are "paradigmatic of the unity of theory and practice" which our liberational theology and ethics espouse.[111] Indeed, our friendships—our relationships with one another, sexual and otherwise—constitute the nexus in which we discover how best to live our lives as gay and lesbian people, the nexus wherein we most fully discern ethical activity as bodyselves in relation.

••••

A Leathersex Case Study: Theory Transforming Practice

••••

True to the dynamic depth in relation that Bob and I try to nurture within our own befriended lives together, Bob astutely commented years ago that I really try to live what I have written, to practice what I preach. Not only do I appreciate his making me consciously reflective about that connection or consistency in my life and work, but lately I have come to realize the prophetic or heuristic function of my writing (theory) for my own life (practice or praxis). Just as I have said to my writing students, the reflective process of working with sources and ideas, of making connections, of writing out those connections, of subjecting our written work to further reflection, and then of revising our written materials enables us to discern what we really think, often for the very first time. It is then, I have discovered, that we have to live up to what we have written; we discern how to live based on what we have thought through. There is a dynamic dialectic as theory and praxis gradually come together, shaping each other along the way.

Although not nearly as systematically as the foregoing, my encounter with and reflections on one specific area of gay male life reflects this dynamic. My brief experience with the overlapping leathersex and S/M communities and my own developing values shaped each other, to the point that many of my ethical conclusions and my decision to relinquish active participation in the leather subculture occurred together over time.[112] In an informal way, then, leathersex serves as a kind of case in point for the ethics of accountability in relation that I am articulating in these pages.

I had only been self-identified and self-ghettoized as a gay man for three or four years when I found myself mesmerized by the group of leathermen who stood together diagonally across the dance floor at my then-favorite gay bar. They looked so unmistakably male. And in finally allowing myself to be gay, I knew that I was not interested in things feminine, which might in some way remind me of my abusive childhood and adolescence as the perennial class sissy. Neither the small-town drag queens nor the more professional, urban female impersonators held any charm for me. I knew I wanted my partner(s)—and, insofar as possible, myself—to be unmistakably male. The *black* leather these men wore, however, disturbed me. Naive as I was, I knew that black leather was associated with sadomasochism (S/M), so I assumed it just meant an inclination to hurting or being hurt. I have a low pain threshold, and I want no part of hurting anybody. I opted for a brown leather

vest and brown cowboy boots, believing that a western look was somehow equally masculine but safer. Then I fell in love with a man wearing
black leather and began to learn differently. I bought another vest—in
black.

I came into leather, then, and into leather sexuality as extensions of
my passion for another man in relationship. The masculine image
enabled me to heal a masculinity battered by classmates, peers, and
even my father—the same masculinity that later, for me as a gay man,
was battered again by church and academia. The passionate sexuality
was an extension of how deeply I felt for a partner in relationship—like
the strong, manly hug by means of which one can almost imagine the
two men fusing into one being. After all, where is the dividing line
whose crossing makes passionate sex "too rough"? Are certain activities
demonstrations of sadomasochism, or yet just other ways for one partner to make love to another?

I was never sure where the definitions began. As my second lover
wanted to explore different ways of making love, I eschewed the label of
"kinky," because I did not think we were—at least not yet. And, at that
point, I began reading everything I could get my hands on. From this
beginning of my entry into the realm of radical sexuality, I realized there
were two schools of thought: the rarified spirituality of a Geoff
Mains[113] and the how-to technique orientation of a Larry Townsend.[114]
I felt right at home with Mains's writing, but did not like the objectification of partners, genitals, and sexuality that I found in Townsend—
any more than I liked the genital reductionism I saw in gay male
pornography. I also did not and still do not like anything that even
remotely resembles dehumanizing, restrictive roles or exploitative
pseudoviolence. While roles consciously and heuristically chosen for a
short period of lovemaking (enabling partners to learn something about
their own innermost selves) might be one thing, any long-term roles
that imitate patriarchal gender roles and thereby restrict another's
humanness have no place in liberation theology or praxis, spirituality, or
life. I also learned that such a leather-spiritual orientation was a minority perspective.

With but few exceptions, I have not engaged in a radical sexual
encounter outside a committed relationship, either with a spouse or

with a very close friend. I have never liked one-night stands or anonymous sexual encounters and have felt that those were not the appropriate situations for the level of trust and knowing (intimacy) that good
leathersex and leather spirituality required. The lover who brought me
into leather ultimately found someone who would go further with him
than I could go. Then, when I became involved with a partner with
whom I was willing to learn more, I still could not feel good about deliv-
ering some of the things he wanted from me. Unlike in the popular folk-
lore, I had come into leather as a "top" first, and things that I had not or
could not experience as a "bottom" did not feel right to me. Some activities just seemed unnecessarily cruel and violent. Certainly, when any
particular technique or group of techniques became more important
than the art and activity of making passionate love with our full bodies,
I found myself increasingly unwilling to participate. This relationship
soon came to an end as well.

In the meantime, I continued to reflect on the message in Mains's
work as well as on the things I was experiencing with my closest
friend—a sexual mentor who was teaching me, not via top/bottom role
play or via objectified techniques, but rather through the extended sessions we engaged in. An equal partner in our teaching and learning
together, he conveyed his far greater experience in ways that enabled us
to make love to each other—in ways that never dehumanized either of
us. During one of our early sessions, we discussed the roles usually
associated with S/M—top/bottom, master/slave, Daddy/boy—and hit on
the notion of the "big brother" who teaches in a different kind of way.
That image has remained an important one for me. This special sexual
friend and mentor was Bob, who subsequently became my spouse; for
in our passion as friends, I found at last the humanizing passion that
unites body and spirit in our lovemaking and in our everyday lives
together.

The interval between purchasing my first article of black leather and
finally discovering the relationship I need also taught me a great deal
about the leather subcommunity—knowledge I might well have done
without. I have realized that my reading of Geoff Mains and my own
writing in this area represent only the most *ideal potential* in radical
sexuality, a potential I have not found realized very often. What I have

found are men who have chosen leather and, more specifically, S/M activities for the wrong reasons. I have seen "bottoms" trapped in roles that repeatedly act out the dysfunctional and sometimes physically or sexually abusive relationships they experienced with their real parents—so trapped that they never find the catharsis that releases them, heals them, and frees them from their painful pasts. I have seen "tops" who use their roles to exploit their partners—who physically abuse their partners, not by way of making love to them but by way of battering them. How many S/M relationships are nothing more than well-constructed facades for spousal abuse of the most dehumanizing kinds?

I have also seen vast numbers of putative leathermen who wear their leather as only a device for attracting sexual partners, as a gimmick in the sexual marketplace. I have witnessed leather pageants where the participants have no more depth than those whose lives are sacrificed in pursuit of any other kind of beauty pageant title. I have watched as leather clubs founded to nurture community get hopelessly mired in politicking and power games, and as their members become obsessed not with siblinghood but with sexual pursuits. I have watched as S/M educational organizations allow their efforts to become narrowly focused on techniques that pay little heed to the quality of relationships, to justice in right relation. I have experienced the ways in which the leathersex and S/M subcommunities discourage long-term, committed couplings. I have observed the ways in which single persons, as well as individuals in open relationships within those subcommunities, shun those in their midst who would make monogamous commitments—mutual and reciprocal commitments in which sexual techniques are necessarily far less important than the overall quality of life together.

Yes, Bob and I still wear some leather on those extremely rare occasions when we go out to the bars to see our friends or to dance. Without being misogynist, the masculine identification is still comforting. The smells and textures of leather enhance our sense of self and the quality of our time "out." The marginality of leather identification reinforces our increasing militancy about the rights of those dispossessed in our society—specifically the rights of persons living with HIV and the rights of all nonheterosexually married couples. Our concerns for inclusion as a people—not by assimilation but in our own right—are underscored by our queerly defiant apparel. At the same time, our sexuality is *not* about techniques or S/M by any means; it is about making love to each other—whether in sex, in cuddling together over our first cup of morning coffee, in sitting together in front of the television exhausted after work, in playing with our dogs, or in working on the yard and garden. Our life together is imbued with our sexuality, but our life together in all its dimensionality is not just about sex, sexual techniques, or our genitals. Our life together and our lives as individuals are far more than that!

My more recent work on the ways in which masculine socialization has shaped gay men's lives and sexuality[115] has caused me to reject adamantly any sexual acting out that reinforces destructive roles, focuses on sexuality as nothing more than a genital function, or fails to enhance the fullest humanity of both partners. When our capacity for being sexual is reduced to certain techniques labeled "S/M" or our capacity for erotic arousal is reduced to certain acceptable costumes labeled "leather," then we have shortchanged ourselves. At the same time, if wearing leather enables us to reclaim and to heal our battered masculinity as gay men while also enabling us to reaffirm *nonsexist* values and behavior, if leather identity engenders in us the nearly lost qualities of respect and good manners, and if leather siblinghood encourages our courageous activity in community in the face of both injustice and AIDS—then our apparel is queerly well chosen. If our passion for our spouses and partners becomes playfully and masculinely rough—embodied equivalents of good "bear hugs" because we love each other *that much*—and if our whole-bodied eroticism enables us to explore all of our bodies and to push our embodied limits together with the power and empowerment of our lovemaking, then our sexuality is truly radical, as it enhances everything about our lives. Our sexuality is also sacramental. Between two men who truly care about each other as friends and/or as spouses, that sacrament may indeed be tremendously powerful, tremendously nurturing and healing, fundamentally humanizing and empowering. Then, of course, what we wear or how we label the ways in which we make love is not *that* important anymore, is it?

So some of my idealism remains intact, not because of accumulated evidence that the majority of people are acting in such a fashion, but rather as a kind of *prophetic hope:* In the hope that all gay men and lesbians in general, as well as those identified with the leather and/or S/M subcommunities, might rise above petty politicking and genital reductionism to reclaim their spiritual potential and embodied holism. In the hope that leather's defiant double marginalization might take heroic embodiment at the forefront of our struggles for the utter liberation of all life. In the hope that all our relationships might indeed embody lovemaking as justice-making. In the hope that we might indeed actualize God-with-us in our erotic and loving passion for one another. Then will we be living accountably in relation, nurturing the friendship that can undergird a truly liberationist ethics capable of nurturing and sustaining life, queerly defiant in the face of death.

$\mathcal{D}$efying the $\mathcal{D}$arkness

The journey through theodicy to ethics reminds us yet again that, for the haunting "why" of suffering and death, there is no utterly satisfying answer that so makes sense of it all as to cancel the pain, the anguish, the grief, and the righteous sense of unfairness we feel in confronting horror and tragedy.[1] Queerly enough, at the very same time, we know in our guts that we must speak against the silence and push against the darkness, ever hoping that something will give, that some grace will emerge from the shadows, and that we will find ourselves empowered to live ethically accountable and queerly defiant lives in relation, in the very face of suffering and even death. So very much of it is up to us. And yet, as relationally embodied selves in a radically horizontal and immanent reality, we are not alone. Our queerly defiant and ethically accountable lives can nurture life-giving companionship even in the midst of seeming godforsakenness.

Ultimately, Kathleen Sands's understanding of tragic consciousness pushes us beyond what we normally think of as tragic—the pathos of Greek or Shakespearean tragedy, Christ's passion—that somehow, despite devastation and incredible suffering, victims will be vindicated. Continuous with Roger Schlobin's and David Blumenthal's work, Sands is actually pressing us toward a horrific consciousness that there may indeed be no vindication, no resurrection, no meaning other than what we create as we "make life go on."[2] Our going on, our very lives lived accountably in relation, becomes a defiant ongoing action in the face of the shadowy ambiguity of divine presence/absence. In short, our queer accountability defies the darkness. Thus, although one way to read our tradition is that God is neither above nor the cause of suffering but empathetically is the one who suffers and the one who strives to ease or overcome suffering, the reality of our experience of Schlobin's monster and Blumenthal's abusive parent/God suggests that such a process-theological reading of the tradition is not so much facile as partial, incomplete. My own demand for completion faces me with a hard question: Am I ready to accept divine implication in suffering? Am I ready to acknowledge that the fullness of the circle of life, the web of being, includes suffering and dying just as surely as it does fecundity and life itself? Or, as Elie Wiesel recommends, am I willing not to defend God any longer (theodicy), but simply to oppose God's enemies?[3] Can I affirm life not only *in spite of* suffering and dying, but *including* suffering and dying? If my choices have been narrowed to either a facile, partial effort to focus only on the positive *or* a celebration of the larger picture, all its foibles intact, I must attempt the latter, no matter how difficult it is now or will be to do so.

However, my willingness to reckon with profound negativity as an inevitable part of reality, as part of my understanding of the immanent and ecosystemically interwoven Divine, does *not* mean that I accept Blumenthal's abusive parent/God. Just because scripture or tradition portrays the Divine as an abusing male, as a patriarchal monster, does not mean that we have to accept such anthropomorphism as an accurate metaphor for the Deity. That "God is abusive, but not always"[4] remains abhorrent and repulsive to me. I will grant holiness and interrelatedness as parts of how I *experience* the Divine, but I will not engage in the error of attributing personality to God in some ontological sense, and certainly not in the sense of the more patriarchal and macho forms of our tradition. I cannot accept an omnipotent and even sometimes capricious, malicious, or tyrannical God; I cannot grant the Divine personality in that sense.

My more holistic and radically immanent theological alternative does not, of course, solve the problem of theodicy. If anything, it simply affirms the ambiguity inherent in our reality: While the radically immanent life energy I think of as God cannot "fix" suffering, cannot protect

us or rescue us, we nevertheless can experience life with all its vulnerability, risks, suffering, and even death as calling out to us, pleading with
us not to give up on it.[5] The Divine also needs us, in and through our
embodied lives in relation. As a result, our primary theological impulse
need not be toward a vertical, hierarchical, heteropatriarchal, and
omnipotent personality, as our tradition contends, but toward a horizontal, radically immanent, thoroughly interdependent holiness that we
experience in pluriform ways—as the circle of life, the web of being, the
Sacred Hoop, as well as an empathetic companion and cosuffering
friend. We realize not so much that God is impotent, but that God simply is not in the rescue business. Rescuing simply is not what the
Divine/cosmos does. Such a companion and interdependent God concept is not a facile alternative, but the acknowledgment of an all-pervading holiness, a panentheistic something that is somehow more than
just the sum of the parts. It is a recognition that *everything is sacred* as
well as a realization that *there is no one and no thing that will rescue us.*
It is up to us, however frustrating and challenging that may be. The
Divine so conceived may be no more worshipworthy than a capricious
omnipotent God. Perhaps worship per se is a vertically hierarchical and
inherently patriarchal activity. So, I do not worship; I do not place the
Divine on a pedestal, separated from the pluriform embodiments of
God that fill our ecosystemic earth. I do pray—to commune, to give
thanks, to hope, to grieve—and I certainly question. Asking questions is
increasingly the shape of my faith.

I keep asking questions because I believe we are entitled to an understanding of the holy (Divine/cosmos), however elusive it may be, which
is, if not all good, at least not maliciously, *willfully* cruel and sadistic—
even sometimes. After all, the abusing parent or spouse is so only "sometimes," but to present oneself continually for more abuse is still patho-
logical. Moreover, how are we to be ethical, to act accountably in relation, if the Divine in Godself is not accountable, but rather is capricious
and even malicious? The impulse within the immanent and interrelated
web of being to enhance the quality of all life is surely a better grounding for accountable ethics. In other words, for me, continually asking
questions is a mode of defiant living in the midst of ambiguity and
abuse, of suffering without rescue. Questioning is resisting. If "silence

equals death," questions nurture life. Our queerly resistant/persistent questioning also defies the darkness. My questions, of course, necessarily return to those two groups who in part compel these reflections. As both someone living with HIV and a theologian working to accept the rightfulness of death in the cycles of life, I am tempted to agree with Sharon Welch that "what is fiercely resisted is not death itself but *untimely death.*"[6] But my questioning impulse persistently wonders whether Granny's experience of diminishment was really any less monstrous for her at ninety than is the suffering and premature death for the person living with AIDS (PWA) at thirty or forty. Both deaths involve suffering and the diminishment of the quality of life; both lives resist the ending of life. If death means pain and suffering at whatever age, do we rightly protest the heightened tragedy of "untimely" death, or is it not somehow facile (as well as ageist) to excuse Granny's dying while bemoaning that of our much younger gay friends?

Facing the reality of suffering as the seemingly necessary end of our lives at whatever age discloses to us again just how strongly resistant we are to seeing God as both companion and monster; as embodied in both the gaybasher and the Nazi as well as in the gay/lesbian and Jewish victims; as both creator and destroyer; as the energies of both predator and prey, life and death; as the absolute yin/yang both/and of good/evil always in tension—and to some extent always capricious to human understanding, to our peculiarly human need for resolution, for some vindication that would assure us that everything, including ourselves, is all right. The challenge we must meet is not only to take responsibility for our lives but to do so without any external divine/cosmic validation. The point is that the inexorable oneness of life/death and good/evil means we are always living in the valley of the shadow of death. Bob's and my experience of the ubiquity of the angel of death vividly reminded us of that reality. Daring to live anyway—to make life go on—is always an act of defiance, of resistance, of protest. Perpetually living in the valley of the shadow of death means perpetually living in defiance of the capriciousness, the pure whimsy, not of God per se, but of *when* suffering and death might come. That is as true for the tenacious elderly or the PWA as for anyone else. To commune with, pray to, and question the immanent energy underlying all that is constitute queer actions of both defiance and embrace. It is saying the "yes" that entails saying "no" to all the abusive "no's" in our lives, including our abusive western religious tradition.

Our two-pronged Judeo-Christian tradition is simply wrong. The tradition has always been so fascinated by a vertical/linear, heteropatriarchally and anthropomorphically conceived Divine—distinct from, even alienated from, the rhythmic cycles of ecosystemically and interrelationally embodied life—that we have blinded ourselves to the horizontal, immanentist, and interconnected wisdom of non-Christian and indigenous peoples. Judeo-Christianity has created many of its own dilemmas, including that of theodicy, by structuring abuse into its anthropomorphic Divine. A post-Christian and ecologically sound view intuits not a hierarchical divine personality, but a horizontal, immanent, interconnected, and interdependent web of life instead. However ultimately impersonal, the cycles of the Sacred Hoop or the circle of life are far less abusive than willfully capricious transcendence. Granted, pain and suffering are still very real. A radically immanent perspective is *not* a panacean view. Predator/prey relations and the ever-changing geosphere alone testify to the violence in the web of being. Importantly, however, that violence is not willfully malicious or gratuitous, not about power or privilege, accumulation or possession. Suffering and death yield new life in an endless circle. Ironically and ambiguously, we experience our lives as linear and mortal within a relational web of being which is cyclical and unending. We humans simply need to be much more careful, responsible, and accountable for what we contribute to or take from that circle—for being abusive or perpetually angry or for being compassionate and life enhancing. Because a tradition built around an abusing male God must surely be anathema for those of us who have suffered abuse at any level, a nonidealized appreciation of nature, a theological position that respects the radically immanent and this-worldly wisdom in the only reality we know, must surely be the more life-affirming stance.

Even with such a perspective, rather than an abusing parent/God concept, the reality of suffering means that a certain healthy distrust of God and a challenging, resisting spirit are still "appropriate religious affections."[7] So, also, is the divinely or cosmically directed anger which

I have so often wrestled with and resisted.[8] One implication of both divine/human mutuality and a relationally embodied theology is that if we get angry with God and do not share that with Godself, we actually risk harming that relationship, much as when we suppress anger in a human relationship and it reemerges in uglier forms as resentment and interpersonal brokenness. Whether a part of the dynamic web of being or the result of human injustice and cruelty, the realities of pain and suffering also mean "the anger of righteous indignation has its place" in our theology.[9] The challenge in our anger is to discern when it is appropriate to direct it toward the Divine/cosmos and when it is appropriate to channel it in ways that transform this-worldly injustice into justice. Relational anger is quite often necessary before forgiveness, reconciliation, and healing are possible. The testimony of the abused reminds us, however, that healing is not the same thing as forgetting, as if the abuse never happened; and it may not even include forgiving, if our conciliatory efforts would only precipitate more abuse. Similarly, healing is not the same as avoiding: Healing requires that we face the darkness—in our lives, in ourselves, in others, and in our society—and push through it and beyond it. Healing is to create redemption for our lives, here and now, independent of any otherworldly, next-worldly validation.

To that end, and even though it feels very uncomfortable in the face of HIV/AIDS or any other chronic, life-threatening condition, I have become increasingly adamant about the very real possibility that this life may indeed be all there is.[10] My commitment to ecological as well as human accountability only strengthens this conviction. Indeed, while the quilted fabric of the web of being is always unraveling and wearing out, it is at the very same time reknitting new combinations—a plaiting together of perishing and possibility.[11] Beyond mere ecological observation, however, I am deeply concerned that otherworldly eschatologies undermine our ethical accountability—toward other human life and certainly toward nonhuman biospheric and geospheric life. An otherworldly eschatology invariably lifts up a "next" world that vitiates or negates both the value of this life and the reality of our experience here, including our suffering. Rather than validating our lives, it ultimately denies their reality. The result is that, in Sands's words:

[The] *absolutization* of the demand for the moral resolution [resurrection, heaven] is inseparable from the refusal of existence as such. To long for the death of death is to long for the death of life. . . . It is wasteful to feign evil's resolution by 'thinking it through to the end,' when what is needed is illumination, creativity, discernment, and transformation in evil's midst.[12]

In other words, any reliance on validation or vindication in a "next" world encourages us to devalue this world and this life—including all the companion life with which we share the present moment—as only penultimate. A truly inclusive liberation theology, therefore, will not be focused on the next world, but will articulate better ways to live in this one: "Were God no longer to secure theology's good ending, perhaps the discipline might create for itself a future in the service of life's going on."[13]

Apart from my theological and ecological concerns, my face-to-face encounter with abuse has also made me aware of a psychological "ulterior motive" in my antieschatological position. The persistent message of abusive parents and our homophobically abusive society to its gay sons and lesbian daughters is that we are "evil," the very evil that Sands asserts is now claiming its right not only to do theology, but to shed the negative label in the process. Unfortunately, all the negative labeling is very effective. We become more adept at tormenting ourselves than anything external to ourselves ever could be. For example, as I have attempted to live in the ambiguity of knowing myself as good and faithful while nevertheless labeled "evil," one means to escape the eschatological hell customarily assigned to those who are evil (the hell to which my father believes I am heading solely because I'm gay) has been to deny heaven as well. My stubborn agnosticism about any possibility of an afterlife has been a part of my flight from the looming darkness, a way to avoid confronting the evil visage in the mirror and the necessity of pushing through it. Now, as I at long last say "no" to the labeling of "evil"—defying and resisting the all-permeating negatives in my life in order to say "yes" to myself—I want to transform my theology. So transformed, my antieschatological theology can shift from an implicitly fearful negation of a next life to the more wholehearted affirmation of the ultimate value of *this* life that it was intended to be all along. It also means at last being able to acknowledge the great unknown as just that and—finally, genuinely—to trust the process beyond this life, however frightening and difficult that may be.[14]

Instead of arguing negatively, fearfully, I now want to argue *for* a marriage of theory and practice—an ethics—that does not depend on an afterlife or on a judging and validating *deus ex machina* as the carrot to compel morally responsible behavior, as either the rationale or motivation for doing whatever we ought to be doing to embody accountability in relation, in relation to *all* life. A post-Bonhoefferian post-Christian, I am doing ethics *as if* God does not exist, *as if* it really is up to us, *as if* this is all there is, *as if* this life and this earth are together of ultimate value. I want myself, my fellow gay men, lesbians, and other persons in general to be humanly and ecologically accountable because both human and nonhuman life matters—because all life matters—and not because "God said so" or because we are either afraid of or desirous of something in the "next" world. I do not want us in any way to dismiss this world as only penultimately valuable! Instead, I want us all to realize that an accountable life also defies the darkness and queerly (re)affirms the ultimate value of *all* life!

Where I need to go in articulating such a defiant mode of living—in articulating the "how"—is well beyond the critical examination of gay male life and sexuality articulated above, however important that remains,[15] and toward a reiteration of the command that we all live humanly compassionate and ecologically accountable lives at one with the circle of life, the Sacred Hoop. That is accountability in relation and an appropriate assumption of embodied responsibility; it is to be engaged in what Rita Nakashima Brock calls "the reconstruction of compassion,"[16] which is clearly an activity more far-reaching than any debilitating obsession with theodicy per se. Blumenthal notes the importance of compassion as our appropriate embodied response to one another: "One of the paths of our lives is walking with the victim—beyond endurance, into suffering that cannot be told—as best we can [and] to confront what we'd rather avoid, with as much courage as we can muster . . . as an act of solidarity [and] an act of remembrance."[17]

Ultimately, I suspect that only by facing the monster—the abusing parent, the internalized label of "evil," the darkness and the ambiguity—and rather than avoiding it, pushing through the darkness, allowing ourselves to experience the painful and frightening exorcism of an accumulated life of naysaying, can we give birth to our best selves, can we finally embrace the wholeness of who we are and say "yes" to ourselves. Then and only then, as self-acknowledged wounded healers, can we find and nurture from our own experiences of woundedness not further acts of wounding, but acts of empathy and compassion, actions that will at last break the cycle of abuse in our lives. Obviously, this is not a once-and-for-all event. We must face down the abuser every time we encounter homophobic societal abuse, every time our parents or their voices internalized in us discount our best efforts, every time we experience pain and suffering and are tempted to project that onto some cosmic being. I face the monster in the mirror daily—both my father's visage and my internalized acceptance of "gay equals evil" and "Michael equals bad"—and I keep pushing against them, through them, screaming my "no" to the "no" at the dark center of my being until the ambiguity of life echoes back my "yes," a "yes" embodied in my own life and in Bob's gracious love which enables me to find the courage and the self-love needed to shout down the darkness. He is the perpetual light at the end of darkness's tunnel, embodying God energy relationally into my life and the life we are creating together.

Over all, I do not want to belittle or demean the Divine by any means or to dismiss the ambivalent both/and of life/death that permeates the web of being; instead, I do want to affirm and to celebrate "life and more life,"[18] even in the middle of the valley of the shadow of death, where the angel of death is as ubiquitous as the radically immanent Divine. I do want to continue to resist the near-at-hand, horrific return of the abusing monster, embodied in HIV in both Bob's and my bodily ecosystems. I do not want to live in terror, nor do I want naively to deny its possibility. Instead, I want both of us to persevere defiantly, courageously, and queerly in the face of that monstrous possibility for a very long time to come. And I want us to continue to discern ecologically sound ways to live creatively in the tension, keeping the ever-present monster at bay while nurturing loving embodied relationships with God and ecosystemic wonder, with our friends and loved ones, knowing full well that life and death, joy and suffering, are one—part and parcel of the whole of reality.

Hope for me then becomes not some neat and linear matter of perfect beginnings and perfect endings, but rather something as multidimensional, dynamic, and even chaotic as everyday life. Or, in Sands's terms, hope is "our messy, multiform continuance. . . . What we need is . . . to mourn and laugh and dance until our flesh remembers how the world goes on."[19] Hope is not eschatologically distant, but here and now, not otherworldly, but resistantly present. Hope also queerly defies the darkness: Hope is our tenacity, our ability to face down the darkness, to live alongside death not with apathy but with empathy and compassion, to assert our "yes" against all the "no's." Our tenacious resistant hope is our celebration of life with all its limitations and problems, the energy of our commitments to accountability and justice, and our embodied relational efforts to enhance the quality of all life. It is indeed the transformative energy of our lives as bodyselves in relation. Such affirmations may constitute a kind of nonhierarchical, nonpatriarchal worship after all. Or they may simply constitute an admonition to do academic theology a little less and, however belatedly, to unabashedly join the dance of life in the great circle of being:

> The divinity that shapes our ends is life, death, and change, understood both literally and as metaphor for our daily lives. . . . There is no promise that life will be other than it is. . . . There will be no end to change, to death, to suffering. But life is as comic as it is tragic. . . . Knowledge that we are but a small part of life and death and transformation is the essential religious insight. The essential religious response is to rejoice and to weep, to sing and to dance . . . in praise of an existence far more complicated, more intricate, more enduring than we are. . . .
>
> It is life that can end in death at any moment that we must love.[20]

Notes

1. Naming the Demons

1. Charlotte Bunch, "A Global Perspective of Feminist Ethics and Diversity," in *Explorations in Feminist Ethics: Theory and Practice*, ed. E. B. Cole and S. Coultrop-McQuinn (Bloomington: Indiana University Press, 1992), 177.

2. Daniel T. Spencer, "From Dislocation to Eco-Location: The Concept of Ecological Location and Autobiography as the Starting Point for Critical Reflection in a Liberationist Ecological Ethic," in *A Rainbow of Religious Studies*, vol. 7 of *Gay Men's Issues in Religious Studies*, ed. J. M. Clark and R. E. Goss (Dallas: Monument Press, 1996), 119–39.

3. Beverly Wildung Harrison, *Making the Connections: Essays in Feminist Social Ethics*, ed. C. S. Robb (Boston: Beacon Press, 1985), 253.

4. Richard L. Rubenstein, *After Auschwitz: Radical Theology and Contemporary Judaism* (Indianapolis: Bobbs-Merrill, 1966), 246.

5. Nelle Morton, *The Journey Is Home* (Boston: Beacon Press, 1985), xxv.

6. J. Michael Clark, *An Unbroken Circle: Ecotheology, Theodicy, and Ethics* (Dallas: Monument Press, 1996), 8–10.

7. J. Michael Clark, "AZT in the Candy Dish, or HIV Conversion as a Right of Passage (Penultimate Reflections)," in *Diary of a Southern Queen: An HIV+ Vision Quest* (Dallas: Monument Press, 1990), 66–97.

8. Robert Goss, *Jesus Acted Up: A Gay and Lesbian Manifesto* (San Francisco: HarperSanFrancisco, 1993), xviii–xxi.

9. Richard P. Hardy, *Knowing the God of Compassion: Spirituality and Persons Living with AIDS* (Ottawa: Novalis, 1993), 68.

10. Ibid., 34, 35.

11. Ibid., 68, 40, 36; cf. 35 (n. 5).

12. Harold Kushner, *Why Bad Things Happen to Good People* (New York: Schocken Books, 1981), 60–61.

13. I could not have dealt with these issues, let alone fashioned their construction into a systematic book-length manuscript, without the help of

some very special and beloved friends and colleagues. Those dearest to me in this process include: Richard Brown, Kenneth Cuthbertson, Richard Hardy, Ron Long, Tina Pippin, and my spouse, Bob McNeir; their valuable insights and comments have significantly enhanced the quality of the final product. I am also indebted to James Doyle of the *Journal of Men's Studies* and to Art James, Belinda Buxjom, and others at Publishers Associates for providing me with earlier forums in which to test many of these ideas (see various citations below). I also want to thank my biology colleague Vicky Finnerty for reminding me several years ago to "trust my instincts"; the recent loss of her husband of thirty-one years has deepened the bond we share around many of these issues. To all these folks who have helped strengthen both my life and my theological voice, I offer my heartfelt thanksgiving.

2. Undermining the Theological Ground

1. J. Michael Clark, "Confessions of Scripture-phobia, or, Why I Don't Use the Bible in My Theology" (unpublished paper, Ideological Criticism Group, Society of Biblical Literature, San Francisco, November 1992). Portions of this presentation subsequently appeared in a very different format and context elsewhere; see: Clark, *An Unbroken Circle*, 22–28. The ensuing discussion is yet a further distillation and elaboration of these ideas.

2. J. Michael Clark, *A Place to Start: Toward an Unapologetic Gay Liberation Theology* (Dallas: Monument Press, 1989), 22–23.

3. Cf. Thomas M. Thurston, "Gay Theology of Liberation and the Hermeneutic Circle," in *Constructing Gay Theology*, vol. 2 of *Gay Men's Issues in Religious Studies*, ed. M. L. Stemmeler and J. M. Clark (Dallas: Monument Press, 1991), 7–26.

4. J. Michael Clark, *Beyond Our Ghettos: Gay Theology in Ecological Perspective* (Cleveland: Pilgrim Press, 1993), 2–3, 4.

5. Anne Primavesi, *From Apocalypse to Genesis: Ecology, Feminism, and Christianity* (Minneapolis: Augsburg Fortress Press, 1991), 231–32, 243.

6. James A. Nash, *Loving Nature: Ecological Integrity and Christian Responsibility* (Nashville: Abingdon Press, 1991), 101.

7. Elie Wiesel, *Messengers of God: Biblical Portraits and Legends*, trans. M. Wiesel (New York: Random House, 1976), 5.

8. For a fictional account from the margins, see: Chinua Achebe, *Things Fall Apart* (London: Heinemann, 1965).

9. Cf. Primavesi, *From Apocalypse to Genesis*, 22; for an extended ecological discussion, see Clark, *Beyond Our Ghettos*.

10. Clark, *Beyond Our Ghettos*, 41–42.

11. Catherine Keller, "Talk about the Weather: The Greening of Eschatology," in *Ecofeminism and the Sacred*, ed. C. J. Adams (New York: Continuum, 1993), 31, 32, 35.

12. Sallie McFague, *The Body of God: An Ecological Theology* (Minneapolis: Augsburg Fortress Press, 1993), 109; Rosemary Radford Ruether, "Ecofeminism: Symbolic and Social Connections of the Oppression of Women and the Domination of Nature," in *Ecofeminism and the Sacred*, ed. Adams, 22.

13. Catherine Keller, "Women against Wasting the World: Notes on Eschatology and Ecology," in *Reweaving the World: The Emergence of Ecofeminism*, ed. I. Diamond and G. F. Orenstein (San Francisco: Sierra Club Books, 1990), 257.

14. Ibid., 260.

15. Ibid., 250, 255.

16. Carol Johnston, "Economics, Eco-Justice, and the Doctrine of God," in *After Nature's Revolt: Eco-Justice and Theology*, ed. D. T. Hessel (Minneapolis: Augsburg Fortress Press, 1992), 154.

17. Keller, "Talk about the Weather," 38.

18. Tina Pippin, *Death and Desire: The Rhetoric of Gender in the Apocalypse of John* (Louisville, Ky.: Westminster/John Knox Press, 1992), 28, 38.

19. Cf. Dee Brown, *Bury My Heart at Wounded Knee: An Indian History of the American West* (1970; reprint, New York: Henry Holt, 1991).

20. Keller, "Talk about the Weather," 47.

21. Ibid., 37, 36.

22. J. Michael Clark, "(Em)Body(d) Theology: Exploring Ecology and Eschatology," *Journal of Men's Studies* 3, no. 1 (August 1994): 73–78.

23. Ronald E. Long, "God through Gay Men's Eyes: Gay Theology in the Age of AIDS," in *AIDS, God, and Faith: Continuing the Dialogue on*

Constructing Gay Theology, ed. R. E. Long and J. M. Clark (Dallas: Monument Press, 1992), 7, 10.

24. Ronald E. Long, "Revisioning and Renewing: A Rejoinder," in *AIDS, God, and Faith,* ed. Long and Clark, 35 (n. 8); cf. 31.

25. Dietrich Bonhoeffer, *Letters and Papers from Prison,* ed. Eberhard Bethge (New York: Macmillan, 1953), 196.

26. Cf. Long, "Revisioning and Renewing," 31.

27. Long, "God through Gay Men's Eyes," 12, 13, 15.

28. Ibid., 13

29. Ibid., 14, 15, 17, 19.

30. Ibid., 20 (n. 7).

31. J. Michael Clark, "Gay Vision and Constructive Theology," in *AIDS, God, and Faith,* ed. Long and Clark, 24.

32. Cf. Hardy, *Knowing the God of Compassion,* 44.

33. Elie Wiesel, *The Trial of God,* trans. M. Wiesel (1979; reprint, New York: Schocken Books, 1986).

34. Ibid., 89; cf. 26, 85.

35. Ibid., 54.

36. Ibid., 123.

37. Ibid., 128.

38. Ibid., 129.

39. Ibid., 156; cf. 132, 133.

40. Ibid., 160–61.

41. Clark, *A Place to Start,* 78.

3. Querying the Divine

1. J. Michael Clark, "AIDS, Death, and God: Gay Liberational Theology and the Problem of Suffering," *Journal of Pastoral Counseling* 21 (1986): 40–54; Clark, *A Place to Start,* 65–78, 164–75; Clark, "(Em)body(d) Theology," 69–86; and J. Michael Clark, "Abuse and Theodicy in Gay Theology and Ethics," *Journal of Men's Studies* 4, no. 2 (November 1995): 111–30. The ensuing discussion is a further distillation of ideas first elucidated in these earlier materials, especially in the more recent work published in the *Journal of Men's Studies.*

2. See: David R. Blumenthal, *Facing the Abusing God: A Theology of Protest* (Louisville, Ky.: Westminster/John Knox Press, 1993).

3. Elie Wiesel, *Night,* trans. S. Rodway (1958; reprint, New York: Avon Books, 1969), 76.

4. Roger C. Schlobin, "Prototypic Horror: The Genre of the Book of Job," *Semeia* 60 (1992): 23.

5. Ibid., 28, 33, 34.

6. Ibid., 31, 33.

7. Ibid., 30; cf. 24; cf. Clark, "(Em)body(d) Theology."

8. Schlobin, "Prototypic Horror," 28; cf. 26–28.

9. Blumenthal, *Facing the Abusing God,* 7, 8, 15–17, 246 ff.

10. Ibid., 16

11. Ibid., 197, 199.

12. Ibid., 197.

13. Ibid., 201.

14. Ibid., 203.

15. James B. Nelson, *Between Two Gardens: Reflections on Sexuality and Religious Experience* (New York: Pilgrim Press, 1983); and James B. Nelson, *The Intimate Connection: Male Sexuality, Masculine Spirituality* (Philadelphia: Westminster Press, 1988); J. Michael Clark, "Men's Studies, Feminist Theology, and Gay Male Sexuality," *Journal of Men's Studies* 1, no. 2 (November 1992): 125–55.

16. J. Michael Clark, *Southern Gothic: Of Remembering and Releasing* (Irving, Tex.: Scholars Books, 1991).

17. Blumenthal, *Facing the Abusing God,* 216; cf. 217, 221.

18. Schlobin, "Prototypic Horror," 235.

19. Kathleen M. Sands, *Escape from Paradise: Evil and Tragedy in Feminist Theology* (Minneapolis: Augsburg Fortress Press, 1994), 1; cf. x.

20. Ibid., 166.

21. Ibid., 8.

22. Ibid., 166.

23. Ibid., 167.

24. See: J. Michael Clark, "Phenomenology and Prophecy, Victimization and Transformation: Further Notes on Gay Ethics," *Journal of Men's Studies* 4, no. 3 (February 1996): 263–79; Ronald E. Long, "The Sacrality of Male Beauty and Homosex: A Neglected Factor in the Understanding of Contemporary Gay Male Life," *Journal of Men's Studies* 4, no. 3 (February 1996): 225–42.

25. Sands, *Escape from Paradise*, 125, 67; cf. 11.
26. Ibid., 12–13, 19.
27. Ibid., 112–13.
28. Ibid., 64.
29. Ibid., 116; cf. 127.
30. Ibid., 96.
31. Ibid., 64.
32. Cf. Clark, "Phenomenology."
33. Sands, *Escape from Paradise*, 85; cf. 143.
34. Clark, "Phenomenology."
35. Sands, *Escape from Paradise*, 159.
36. Clark, "Phenomenology."

4. Doing Gay Ethics

1. McFague, *The Body of God*, 18.
2. Cf. J. Michael Clark, *A Lavender Cosmic Pilgrim: Further Ruminations on Gay Spirituality, Theology, and Sexuality* (Las Colinas, Tex.: The Liberal Press, 1990), 7–14.
3. McFague, *The Body of God*, 16.
4. Harrison, *Making the Connections*, 13, 114; cf. 258.
5. Carol S. Robb, "Introduction," in Harrison, *Making the Connections*, xix.
6. James Nelson, *Body Theology* (Louisville, Ky.: Westminster/John Knox Press, 1992), 43; cf. 45, 116–17.
7. Robb, "Introduction," xix–xx.
8. Mary E. Hunt, *Fierce Tenderness: A Feminist Theology of Friendship* (New York: Crossroad, 1991), 131; cf. 156.
9. Robb, "Introduction," xvi.
10. Eve Browning Cole and Susan Coultrop-McQuinn, "Toward a Feminist Conception of Moral Life," in *Explorations in Feminist Ethics*, ed. Cole and Coultrop-McQuinn, 8.
11. Linda A. Bell, *Rethinking Ethics in the Midst of Violence: A Feminist Approach to Freedom* (Lanham, Md.: Rowman & Littlefield, 1993), 17.
12. Margaret Urban Walker, "Moral Understandings: Alternative 'Epistemology' for a Feminist Ethics," in *Explorations in Feminist Ethics*, ed. Cole and Coultrop-McQuinn, 170–71.

13. Robb, "Introduction," xv.

14. Sheila D. Collins, "Theology in the Politics of Appalachian Women," in *WomanSpirit Rising: A Feminist Reader*, ed. C. P. Christ and J. Plaskow (San Francisco: Harper & Row, 1979), 152.

15. Walker, "Moral Understandings," 171,

16. J. Michael Clark, "From Gay Men's Lives: Toward a More Inclusive, Ecological Vision," *Journal of Men's Studies* 1, no. 4 (May 1993): 357.

17. Harrison, *Making the Connections*, 244.

18. Sharon D. Welch, *A Feminist Ethic of Risk* (Minneapolis: Fortress Press, 1990), 133; cf. 137, 145.

19. Ibid., 35; Bunch, "A Global Perspective," 180.

20. Bunch, "A Global Perspective," 180, 181.

21. Ibid., 181.

22. Bell, *Rethinking Ethics*, 73; cf. 72.

23. Welch, *A Feminist Ethic of Risk*, 38, 126.

24. Ibid., 35.

25. Walker, "Moral Understandings," 172; cf. Sarah Lucia Hoagland, "Lesbian Ethics and Female Agency," in *Explorations in Feminist Ethics*, ed. Cole and Coultrop-McQuinn, 157–58.

26. Harrison, *Making the Connections*, 15, 16.

27. Ibid., 11, 12, 17–18.

28. Ibid., 18.

29. Welch, *A Feminist Ethic of Risk*, 173.

30. Ibid., 174, 162, 161; cf. Harrison, *Making the Connections*, 18–19.

31. Hoagland, "Lesbian Ethics and Female Agency," 162–63.

32. Long, "God through Gay Men's Eyes," 14.

33. Welch, *A Feminist Ethic of Risk*, 10.

34. Bell, *Rethinking Ethics*, 79; cf. McFague, *The Body of God*, 8.

35. The most noteworthy exceptions regarding an analysis of antigay/antilesbian oppression and violence, respectively, include: John E. Fortunato, *Embracing the Exile: Healing Journeys of Gay Christians* (New York: Seabury Press, 1983), and, Gary David Comstock, *Violence against Lesbians and Gay Men* (New York: Columbia University Press, 1991).

36. Welch, *A Feminist Ethic of Risk*, 15.

37. Ibid., 93, 94.

38. Cf. Bell, *Rethinking Ethics*, 77–78.
39. Welch, *A Feminist Ethic of Risk*, 14.
40. Michael Callen, "The Finale," *Genre* (March 1994): 75.
41. Welch, *A Feminist Ethic of Risk*, 70, 19.
42. Ibid., 75.
43. Harrison, *Making the Connections*, 249, 250.
44. Welch, *A Feminist Ethic of Risk*, 154–55; cf. 139.
45. Ibid., 79–80, 22.
46. Ibid., 77.
47. Ibid., 20.
48. Harrison, *Making the Connections*, 14–15.
49. Ibid., 14.
50. Hunt, *Fierce Tenderness*, 19; cf. 77, 147, 95, 96.
51. Ibid., 89.
52. Harrison, *Making the Connections*, 11.
53. J. Michael Clark, *A Defiant Celebration: Theological Ethics and Gay Sexuality* (Garland, Tex.: Tangelwuld Press, 1990).
54. Ronald E. Long, "An Affair of Men: Masculinity and the Dynamics of Gay Sex," *Journal of Men's Studies* 3, no. 1 (August 1994): 23, 40.
55. Ibid., 25, 32.
56. Ibid., 33.
57. Ronald E. Long, "Gay Theology: Almost Home" (unpublished paper, Gay Men's Issues in Religion Group, American Academy of Religion, Chicago, November 1994), 17.
58. Long, "An Affair of Men," 45 (n. 12), 40.
59. Long, "Gay Theology," 19, 17.
60. Cf. Long, "An Affair of Men," 27ff; and Long, "Gay Theology," 18.
61. Cf. Long, "An Affair of Men," 42–43.
62. Jay E. Johnson, "From the Pineal Gland to the Hypothalamus: Reconstructing (Inevitable) Essentialism in Cultural and Theological Categories" (unpublished paper, Gay Men's Issues in Religion Group, American Academy of Religion, Chicago, November 1994), 6.
63. Cf. Long, "An Affair of Men," 24, 25.
64. Daniel T. Spencer, "Constructing Theology and Ethics: Response" (unpublished paper, Gay Men's Issues in Religion Group, American Academy of Religion, Chicago, November 1994). I also deeply appreci-

ate my informal conversations with Dan in regard to the issues discussed during this meeting; his remarks contributed significantly to my final approach to Long's work.

65. Rosemary Radford Ruether, *Liberation Theology* (New York: Paulist Press, 1972), 13, 16, 32, 34.

66. Welch, *A Feminist Ethic of Risk*, 109; cf. 106.

67. Cf. Cole and Coultrop-McQuinn, "Toward a Feminist Conception of Moral Life," 7.

68. Bell, *Rethinking Ethics*, 20, 29–30.

69. Carter Heyward, *Touching Our Strength: The Erotic as Power and the Love of God* (San Francisco: Harper, 1989), 41.

70. Earl E. Shelp, "AIDS, High Risk Behaviors, and Moral Judgments," in *Sexuality and the Sacred: Sources for Theological Reflection*, ed. J. B. Nelson and S. P. Longfellow (Louisville, Ky.: Westminster/John Knox Press, 1994), 317, 321.

71. Ibid., 318–19.

72. Harrison, *Making the Connections*, 139, 140; cf. 141.

73. J. Michael Clark with Bob McNeir, *Masculine Socialization and Gay Liberation: A Conversation on the Work of James Nelson and Other Wise Friends* (Las Colinas, Tex.: The Liberal Press, 1992); and, Clark, "Men's Studies," 125–55; the ensuing discussion highlights issues examined in detail in these previously published resources.

74. Callen, "The Finale," 44, 46.

75. Callen, *Surviving AIDS* (New York: HarperCollins, 1990), 2–3; cf. Callen, "The Finale," 90.

76. Callen, *Surviving AIDS*, 12 (n. 5), 4.

77. Callen, "The Finale," 47.

78. Callen, *Surviving AIDS*, 4.

79. Ibid., 6.

80. Callen, "The Finale," 74, 75.

81. Ibid., 47.

82. Ibid., 44.

83. Callen, *Surviving AIDS*, 2, 10.

84. Ibid., 187; cf. 2, 4, 10.

85. Cf. Walker, "Moral Understandings," 165–66.

86. Cf. Alison M. Jaggar, "Feminist Ethics: Projects, Problems, Prospects,"

in *Feminist Ethics,* ed. C. Card (Lawrence: University of Kansas Press, 1991), 98, 99; Rosemary Radford Ruether, "Homophobia, Heterosexism, and Pastoral Practice," in *Sexuality and the Sacred,* ed. Nelson and Longfellow, 391. Ironically, perhaps, the first voice to adamantly oppose any gay/straight double standards in sexual ethics was that of a nongay men's studies scholar and ethicist, James B. Nelson, who elaborated:

> The appropriate ethical question is this: What sexual behavior will serve and enhance, rather than inhibit and damage, the fuller realization of divinely intended humanity? The answer . . . is sexual behavior in accordance with love . . . commitment, trust, tenderness, respect for the other, and the desire for responsible communion. It means resisting cruelty, utterly impersonal sex, obsession with sexual gratification, and actions that display unwillingness to take responsibility for their personal and social consequences. *This kind of ethic is equally appropriate to both heterosexual and homosexual. . . .*
>
> What can be said to everyone regardless of [sexual] orientation is this: genital expression will find its greatest fulfillment in a relationship of ongoing commitment and communion.

See Nelson, *Between Two Gardens,* 124 (emphasis added).
87. Cf. Clark, *Beyond Our Ghettos.*
88. Cf. Bunch, "A Global Perspective," 179–80.
89. Callen, *Surviving AIDS,* 14–15 (n. 14).
90. Harrison, *Making the Connections,* 149; Callen himself confesses, "Back then, I always admired anyone who actually found intimacy sexy." See: Surviving AIDS, 153.
91. Heyward, *Touching Our Strength;* Nelson, *Body Theology, Between Two Gardens;* and Nelson, *The Intimate Connection;* cf. n. 86, above.
92. Cf. Clark, *A Defiant Celebration,* 53; J. Michael Clark, "Men's Studies," in *Sexuality and the Sacred,* ed. Nelson and Longfellow, 225, 226.
93. Heyward, *Touching Our Strength,* 131.
94. Ibid., 129–33.

95. Ibid., 136.
96. Hunt, *Fierce Tenderness*, 49, 82.
97. J. Michael Clark, "Monasticism, Homoeroticism, and St. Aelred," in *Gay Being, Divine Presence: Essays in Gay Spirituality* (Garland, Tex.: Tangelwuld Press, 1987), 48–54.
98. Kath Weston, *Families We Choose: Lesbians, Gays, Kinship* (New York: Columbia University Press, 1991); Hunt, *Fierce Tenderness*. For a review of Weston's text, see J. Michael Clark, *Gay Affirmative Ethics*, vol. 4 of *Gay Men's Issues in Religious Studies*, ed. M. L. Stemmeler and J. M. Clark (Dallas: Monument Press, 1993), 125–29.
99. Hunt, *Fierce Tenderness*, 102, 103.
100. Harrison, *Making the Connections*, 253.
101. Hunt, *Fierce Tenderness*, 100; indeed, genuine mutuality and intimacy enhance the individuals in relation and never require the dissolution of that individuality, as James B. Nelson has reiterated:

> Authentic sexual communion with a beloved human partner . . . is unity, though not unification. Each self respects the other's identity and, in the ecstasy of mutual giving and receiving, creative differences remain . . .
> Relational power understands that the capacity to absorb the influence of another without losing the self's own center is as truly a quality of power as is the strength of exerting influence on another.

See Nelson, *Between Two Gardens*, 11; and Nelson, *The Intimate Connection*, 102.
102. Hunt, *Fierce Tenderness*, 104, 99, 151, 171.
103. Ibid., 108, 151, 163, 29.
104. Ibid., 81, 163, 171.
105. Ibid., 53, 72.
106. Cf. ibid., 131.
107. Ibid., 28; cf. Harrison, *Making the Connections*, 107–10.
108. Hunt, *Fierce Tenderness*, 137, 139.
109. Ibid., 133.

110. Cf. ibid., 72.
111. Ibid., 4, 7, 69, 105.
112. In chronological order as they were *written* (not as they were *published*) see: J. Michael Clark, *Theologizing Gay: Fragments of Liberation Activity* (Oak Cliff, Tex.: Minuteman Press, 1991), 15–19; Clark, *A Defiant Celebration*, 83–93; Clark, *A Lavender Cosmic Pilgrim*, 68–78; and J. Michael Clark, "Radical Reflections on Radical Sexuality," *White Crane*, no. 12 (1992), 4–7, 17 (reprinted in *Sex and Spirit: Exploring Gay Men's Spirituality*, ed. R. Barzan [San Francisco: White Crane Press, 1995], 37–43).
113. Geoff Mains, *Urban Aboriginals: A Celebration of Leathersexuality* (San Francisco: Gay Sunshine Press, 1984).
114. Larry Townsend, *The Leatherman's Handbook II* (New York: Modernismo, 1983).
115. Clark with McNeir, *Masculine Socialization and Gay Liberation*; Clark, "Men's Studies."

5. Defying the Darkness

1. Clark, *A Place to Start*, 174.
2. Cf. Sands, *Escape from Paradise*, 169.
3. Wiesel, *The Trial of God*, 156.
4. Blumenthal, *Facing the Abusing God*, 247; cf. 242.
5. Cf. ibid., 230.
6. Welch, *A Feminist Ethic of Risk*, 159.
7. Blumenthal, *Facing the Abusing God*; 235; cf. 253, 257.
8. Clark, "(Em)body(d) Theology," 79–81.
9. Blumenthal, *Facing the Abusing God*, 18.
10. Cf. Clark, "(Em)body(d) Theology."
11. Cf. Sands, *Escape from Paradise*, 168; cf. Clark, *An Unbroken Circle*, 171–77.
12. Sands, *Escape from Paradise*, 29.
13. Ibid., 36.
14. Cf. Rosemary Radford Ruether, *Gaia and God: An Ecofeminist Theology of Earth Healing* (San Francisco: HarperSanFrancisco, 1992).

15. Cf. J. Michael Clark, "Profeminist Men's Studies and Gay Ethics," *Journal of Men's Studies* 3, no. 3 (February 1995): 241–55; and Clark, "Phenomenology."

16. Rita Nakashima Brock, Foreword, in Blumenthal, *Facing the Abusing God*, xii.

17. Blumenthal, *Facing the Abusing God*, 54.

18. Long, "God through Gay Men's Eyes," 19.

19. Sands, *Escape from Paradise*, 169.

20. Carol P. Christ, "Rethinking Theology and Nature," in *Weaving the Visions: New Patterns in Feminist Spirituality*, ed. J. Plaskow and C. P. Christ (San Francisco: Harper & Row, 1989), 321, 322.

Selected Bibliography

Bell, Linda A. *Rethinking Ethics in the Midst of Violence: A Feminist Approach to Freedom*. Lanham, Md.: Rowman & Littlefield, 1993.

Blumenthal, David R. *Facing the Abusing God: A Theology of Protest*. Louisville, Ky.: Westminster/John Knox Press, 1993.

Callen, Michael. "The Finale." *Genre* (March 1994): 44, 46–47, 74–75, 90.

———. *Surviving AIDS*. New York: HarperCollins, 1990.

Card, Claudia, ed. *Feminist Ethics*. Lawrence: University of Kansas Press, 1991.

Clark, J. Michael. *Beyond Our Ghettos: Gay Theology in Ecological Perspective*. Cleveland: Pilgrim Press, 1993.

———. *A Defiant Celebration: Theological Ethics and Gay Sexuality*. Garland, Tex.: Tangelwuld Press, 1990.

———. *Diary of a Southern Queen: An HIV+ Vision Quest*. Dallas: Monument Press, 1990.

———. *A Lavender Cosmic Pilgrim: Further Ruminations on Gay Spirituality, Theology, and Sexuality*. Las Colinas, Tex.: The Liberal Press, 1990.

———. *A Place to Start: Toward an Unapologetic Gay Liberation Theology*. Dallas: Monument Press, 1989.

———. *An Unbroken Circle: Ecotheology, Theodicy, and Ethics*. Dallas: Monument Press, 1996.

Clark, J. Michael, with Bob McNeir. *Masculine Socialization and Gay Liberation: A Conversation on the Work of James Nelson and Other Wise Friends*. Las Colinas, Tex.: The Liberal Press, 1992.

Clark, J. Michael, and Daniel T. Spencer, eds. "Gay Men's Issues in Religious Studies: A Special Issue." *Journal of Men's Studies* 4, no. 3 (February 1996).

Cole, Eve Browning, and Susan Coultrop-McQuinn, eds. *Explorations in Feminist Ethics: Theory and Practice*. Bloomington: University of Indiana Press, 1992.

Goss, Robert. *Jesus Acted Up: A Gay and Lesbian Manifesto*. San Francisco: HarperSanFrancisco, 1993.

Hardy, Richard P. *Knowing the God of Compassion: Spirituality and Persons Living with AIDS*. Ottawa: Novalis, 1993.

Harrison, Beverly Wildung. *Making the Connections: Essays in Feminist Social Ethics*. Edited by C. S. Robb. Boston: Beacon Press, 1985.

Heyward, Carter. *Touching Our Strength: The Erotic as Power and the Love of God*. San Francisco: Harper, 1989.

Hunt, Mary E. *Fierce Tenderness: A Feminist Theology of Friendship*. New York: Crossroad, 1991.

Kushner, Harold. *Why Bad Things Happen to Good People*. New York: Schocken Books, 1981.

Long, Ronald E. "An Affair of Men: Masculinity and the Dynamics of Gay Sex." *Journal of Men's Studies* 3, no. 1 (August 1994): 21–48.

Long, Ronald E., and J. Michael Clark. *AIDS, God, and Faith: Continuing the Dialogue on Constructing Gay Theology*. Dallas: Monument Press, 1992.

Mains, Geoff. *Urban Aboriginals: A Celebration of Leathersexuality*. San Francisco: Gay Sunshine Press, 1984.

Nelson, James B. *Between Two Gardens: Reflections on Sexuality and Religious Experience*. New York: Pilgrim Press, 1983.

———. *Body Theology*. Louisville, Ky.: Westminster/John Knox Press, 1992.

———. *The Intimate Connection: Male Sexuality, Masculine Spirituality*. Philadelphia: Westminster Press, 1988.

Nelson, James B., and Sandra P. Longfellow, eds. *Sexuality and the Sacred: Sources for Theological Reflection*. Louisville, Ky.: Westminster/John Knox Press, 1994.

Sands, Kathleen M. *Escape from Paradise: Evil and Tragedy in Feminist Theology*. Minneapolis: Augsburg Fortress Press, 1994.

Schlobin, Roger C. "Prototypic Horror: The Genre of the Book of Job." *Semeia* 60 (1992): 23–38.

Stemmeler, Michael L., and J. Michael Clark, eds. *Constructing Gay Theology*. Dallas: Monument Press, 1991.

———. *Gay Affirmative Ethics*. Dallas: Monument Press, 1993.

Welch, Sharon D. *A Feminist Ethic of Risk*. Minneapolis: Fortress Press, 1990.

Wiesel, Elie. *The Trial of God*. Trans. M. Wiesel. New York: Schocken Books, 1979, 1986.

Index

abuse, 29, 93–95; and ambiguity of self as good and evil, 35–39; cycle of, 33–34; God as abusive parent, 31–35, 88; God as monster, 29–31, 88; internalization of, 37; tragic-horrific theology and, 39–42, 87

accountability: case study of, 80–86; prophecy and, 64–73; in relation, 73–80; as resistance, 72–73; solidarity and, 47

Aelred (Saint), 77

afterlife, 16–17, 92–94

agnosticism, 93

AIDS/HIV: affirmation of life and, 5–8; anger and, 22–23; apocalypticism and, 18; blaming victims of, 65–66; compassion and, 49–50; fear of, 2–3; impasse of, 7–8; living with, 5–6; long-term survival of, 68; medical politics of, 71; moral issues of, 74; as natural evil, 41; presence of God and, 29–31; revaluing the bodyself and, 44; setting up for, 67–68, 70–72; single cause/single treatment approach, 71–72; theodicy of, 6–7; untimely death and, 90; violence of, 2–3

alternatively objective ethics, 46–47

Alves, Rubem, 22

American Indians, 17

anger, 22–25, 57–58, 91–92

anthropomorphism, 91

apocalypticism, 15–18

assimilation, 38, 48, 52–53, 56

AZT, 71

Bible. *See* scripture

blaming the victim, 65–66

Blumenthal, David, 31, 34–35, 39, 87–88, 94

bodyselves, 43–44; revaluing, 44–45; right relation and, 45–49

Bonhoeffer, Dietrich, 21, 39, 94

both/and concept, 46, 47, 54, 79, 95

Brock, Rita Nakashima, 94

Bryant, Anita, 54

Bunch, Charlotte, 3–4

Callen, Michael, 54, 59, 68–75

canon. *See* scripture

caregiving, 49–51

center/margins hierarchy, 14

certainty, 71

choices, 50–51

circle of being, 96

circle of life, 56, 89, 91, 94

civil rights, 48

Clark, J. Michael, 23

community, 10, 37–38, 80

About the Author

J. Michael Clark (Ph.D., 1983) is an interdisciplinary adjunct faculty member at Emory University, Georgia State University, and Agnes Scott College, teaching religion and ecology as well as first-year English. He is also cofounder of the Gay Men's Issues in Religion Group of the American Academy of Religion, serving as its cochair from 1987 to 1993. He serves on the editorial board of the *Journal of Men's Studies*. He lives with his spouse, Bob McNeir, and their "family" of dogs, birds, fishpond, flower and vegetable gardens on a hill overlooking downtown Atlanta. He is the author of more than two dozen articles in gay studies. This is his fourteenth book.